The Quiet Disorders of the Mind and the Art of Clear Thinking

A Study of Common Mental Troubles and the Principles That Restore Intellectual Balance

The Quiet Disorders

of the

Mind and the Art of Clear Thinking

A Study of Common Mental Troubles and the Principles That Restore Intellectual Balance

(Illustrated, Refined & Edited)

By. J. Mortimer-Granville

Beyond Books Hub

Books Beyond Imagination

Beyond Books Hub
Books Beyond Imagination

Publication Year: **2026** | Publisher: **Beyond Books**
ISBN: **9789377070854**

Edition: **First Edition, 2026** | Contact: **ddsalesglobal@gmail.com**

Book Name: **The Quiet Disorders of the Mind and the Art of Clear Thinking**
Author: J.**Mortimer-Granville**
Price**: Rs 300/-**

Table of Content

Part-2
The Inner Architecture of a Clear and Steady Mind

Reader's Note

This book is not concerned with rare or dramatic forms of mental illness, nor does it speak to the sensational edges of psychological disorder. Its subject is far closer, far quieter, and therefore far more important: the subtle disturbances of thought and feeling that visit ordinary, capable, conscientious people—often without warning, and frequently without explanation.

Most readers will recognize themselves somewhere in these pages. The chapters describe experiences that do not announce themselves as illness, yet steadily erode confidence, clarity, and joy: the mind that cannot rest, the memory that fails at critical moments, the sudden invasion of fear without cause, the exhaustion that follows thought itself, the sense of being overwhelmed by one's own consciousness. These are not failures of intelligence or character; they are conditions of strain, imbalance, and misdirection—conditions that modern life quietly multiplies.

Part One, *The Hidden Struggles of the Human Mind,* gives language to what many feel but cannot name. Each chapter isolates a specific mental burden—disordered thinking, sleepless reflection, faltering speech, low spirits, languor, fear—and examines it with patience, sympathy, and precision. The value of these chapters lies not only in explanation, but in recognition. To see one's own difficulty clearly described is often the first step toward relief. Part Two, *The Inner Architecture of a Clear and Steady Mind,* moves beyond diagnosis to restoration. It does not promise shortcuts, techniques, or artificial optimism. Instead, it reveals how clarity is built: through understanding habit, regulating mental energy, correcting false ideas about time and pleasure, moderating self-importance, and recovering simplicity of aim. These chapters show that a clear head is not a gift reserved for the fortunate, but a condition shaped by principles that can be learned, practiced, and sustained.

This book rewards attentive reading. It is thoughtful without being heavy, serious without being bleak, and practical without being simplistic. It offers intellectual stimulation alongside genuine comfort, and it respects the reader as a thinking, feeling human being rather than a problem to be fixed.

Those who seek mental sharpness without harshness, discipline without rigidity, and understanding without jargon will find this work both bracing and companionable. It is a book to return to—not for answers alone, but for orientation.

Editor's Preface

The author of this concise yet thoughtful work, Dr. Joseph Mortimer-Granville, may not be widely familiar to contemporary American readers, but in his own time he held a respected position within the medical and intellectual circles of London. He was particularly regarded for his careful study of disorders of the mind and for the seriousness with which he approached questions of mental health long before they became matters of public discussion.

Between the years 1875 and 1877, Dr. Mortimer-Granville was entrusted by the proprietors of *The Lancet* with the task of conducting a detailed investigation into the organization, management, and treatment practices of English lunatic asylums. His findings were published serially in that influential journal and later expanded into a substantial two-volume work entitled *The Care and Cure of the Insane*. This publication significantly strengthened his professional standing and confirmed his reputation as a thoughtful and independent observer.

What distinguishes Dr. Mortimer-Granville from many physicians of his specialty is the attention he devoted to the earliest and most subtle signs of mental disturbance. While others focused chiefly on advanced and unmistakable illness, he recognized that the beginnings of mental disorder are often quiet, gradual, and easily overlooked. His supervision of the second edition of Dr. Wynter's *Borderlands of Insanity* reflects this concern, and it was directly from such observations that the present work emerged.

This book is addressed not to specialists alone, but to the general reader. It is intended as a practical guide to the hygiene of the mind. It examines those common mental difficulties and weaknesses from which few people are entirely free—conditions that quietly diminish intellectual efficiency and emotional balance, and which, in certain dispositions, may develop into serious mental alienation if they are not recognized and corrected in time.

Dr. Mortimer-Granville places strong emphasis on the power of the will. He holds that many of these mental troubles can be overcome when the will is intelligently directed at their earliest appearance. In an age increasingly inclined to view human beings as mere physiological mechanisms, to regard thought as nothing more than a function of the brain, and to attribute mental suffering almost entirely to bodily disorder, it is both bracing and reassuring to encounter a physician of wide experience who firmly affirms the mind's capacity to govern itself. He speaks with conviction of self-control and self-government as essential elements in both the prevention and treatment of mental disease.

His writings, particularly the two essays reprinted in this volume, achieved rapid and widespread popularity and have undoubtedly been of genuine benefit to many readers.

He himself explains that these two works—*Common Mind-Troubles* and *The Secret of a Clear Head*—are in reality parts of a single, unified treatise, and for this reason they are presented together here. Their purpose is to explain how the mind may be wisely cared for and trained amid the ordinary strains and pressures of daily life; how its most frequent disturbances may question is how the visible wrong came into being. If, fortunately, the failing is detected at an early stage, before it has produced conspicuous harm, we may ask more profitably: what forces are at work, where do they operate, and how can they be checked? Why does one person show a tendency toward excessive indulgence in drink or uncontrolled passion, while another seems unable to recognize or pursue the right and honest course whenever temptation or difficulty arises?

It is both reasonable and useful to search for the causes and conditions that shape these failings. Many shortcomings that are commonly regarded as beyond remedy might be amended, and even entirely removed, if the will were resolutely directed, with the aid of experience and scientific insight, to discover their hidden sources. Weakness, pliability, subjection to passion, moral distortion, or an apparent lack of principle often have roots that can be traced and confronted. Alongside these stand defects less severely judged but no less destructive—indolence, lack of perseverance, and indifference to truth. Together, these form, or themselves constitute, what the careless and the unreflective dismiss as mere "failings."

Some of the most regrettable and damaging failings that stain and discredit character appear repeatedly within families, passing from one generation to another and seeming to be inherited. This fact is well established and has been cited as decisive proof of the theory that mind, and therefore character, is nothing more than a product of matter. The argument rests on the assumption that only material elements can be transmitted from parent to child; that a particular structure of the brain and nervous system, a certain arrangement of the physical components of the mental organ, may be reproduced, and that similarity of character must necessarily follow. From this standpoint, the independent existence of mind or spirit is dismissed as a fiction, destined, it is claimed, to be swept away by advancing science, and clung to only by thinkers hampered by prejudice.

Let us examine this claim more closely. It is often stated that all we know of mind is expressed and understood through physical processes and the language of material force. Thought is communicated by speech, and we commonly think in words. The ability to form and use words is known to depend on the brain. Injury or disease affecting certain regions of the brain frequently destroys the power of speech. From such facts, the materialist concludes that mind is produced by matter. What is overlooked is that the only conclusion justified by these observations is that mind, or spirit, expresses itself through the brain as its instrument.

To deny the independent existence of mind on this basis is no more reasonable than to deny the existence or skill of a musician because he cannot perform a full orchestral score on a single flute. The brain is the organ of thought, just as the instrument is the medium of music. Without it, intellectual work cannot be performed, but its necessity does not disprove the reality of the mind any more than the need for an instrument disproves the existence of the artist.

The capacity of the instrument certainly limits expression, but it does not measure the power or ability of the performer, except insofar as the instrument is badly used. This exception is significant and deserves attention elsewhere. For the present, it is enough to recognize that while brain power determines the manner in which mind is manifested, it neither measures nor confirms nor refutes the independent existence of mind itself. Anatomists, physiologists, and chemists rightly confess that they cannot discover a soul within the physical organism. This failure no more disproves its existence than the inability to detect unknown planets at a given stage of astronomy proved that no others existed.

History and experience alike warn us against denying what we do not yet fully understand. It is especially unscientific to reject the existence of a psychical power operating in or through the physical nature of humanity, when it is precisely this hypothesis that enables us to explain some of the most familiar and clearly observed facts of mind and character. Consider, for example, two individuals whose brains are microscopically similar in structure and equal in weight. Both are highly developed, and any differences detectable by the most refined scientific tests are known to be functionally insignificant. Their surroundings and life circumstances offer no explanation for their differences. Yet the moral character of one proves wholly corrupt, while that of the other is conspicuously upright. How can such a contrast be explained except by recognizing the existence of a soul, an inner power that cannot be reduced to matter alone?

There is scarcely any fallacy more widespread, and yet more entirely unfounded, than the belief that virtue or vice can be reliably associated with particular forms of physical or intellectual development.

It is true that there are degrees of animal excellence, and that the lower forms of life tend more readily toward brutality. But the highest and most refined development is not only compatible with grave moral defects; it is often found in close alliance with them. The most delicate and efficient instrument may be turned to the worst purposes. What, then, determines the outcome? Why does one person, endowed with the highest intellectual organization, become an unscrupulous wrongdoer, a menace to society, and a reproach to humanity, while another, whose physical organism is so nearly identical that science can detect no difference, displays qualities of an entirely opposite kind? The superficial answer to this searching question is commonly framed in a single word: circumstances.

Education, example, opposition, health, and other influences of environment are said to have made the difference. Yet this explanation collapses when tested by experience. A review of lives personally known to any thoughtful observer will show that those who have been nurtured with the greatest care often stray far from the right path, while others, neglected and seemingly corrupted by adverse conditions, rise above their surroundings and attain the highest moral development.

The appeal against materialism rests upon the instinct of common sense. If mind were nothing more than a product of matter, science would long ago have discovered some fairly constant relation between peculiarities of physical structure and manifestations of character. Instead, each advance in research tends to disprove any fixed dependence between moral qualities and material conditions. Even the supposed connections relied upon by physiognomists and phrenologists have proved illusory, except in so far as they may represent effects rather than causes of character. Facial expression, for example, is often shaped by education and habit, as is clearly seen in the case of criminals. The notion of a criminal shape of skull has been abandoned, much like the crude belief that guilt can be detected by a "hang-dog" or "murderous" look.

Failings must be examined in the light of these facts. The moral issue at stake is one of responsibility for the use each person makes of the mental power entrusted to him. To neglect one's gifts and capacities is, ethically, as serious a fault as to employ them for harmful ends. The servant who buried his talent was held accountable not for misuse, but for failure to use it. That parable expresses a truth of profound practical importance. We are responsible for developing our faculties through exercise. If they are allowed to lie dormant or remain rudimentary, the resulting deficiencies and failings are our own fault, and no valid excuse can be offered.

The obligation to act in accordance with known duty cannot be evaded. A failing is an act of disregard for the law that development comes through use.

It is disobedience to a command that is clearly understood. The very fact that a failing is recognized gives it the character of an offence. There may, indeed, be shortcomings in the execution of a worthy resolve. Few human efforts achieve complete success at once. Yet failure that occurs in the course of earnest and well-directed effort is not so much a fault as a limitation.

Progress is made by successive advances. The rising tide reaches its height through repeated movements. Self-improvement follows the same law.

The force of persistent effort accumulates, moving steadily forward, though each advance may seem small and incomplete when viewed in isolation.

Failings, as here considered, are faults in character that are habitually excused and that the individual makes no serious attempt to correct. Some of these, as noted earlier, are inherited, and on this account they often receive sympathy rather than blame. In truth, they are the least pardonable. When a defect is known to have been transmitted from parent to child, the latter usually has before him a living example of its consequences. If the failing takes the form of a vicious tendency, its ugliness may be recalled as a warning, stimulating both will and conscience to remove it. If it is a deficiency such as indolence, lack of perseverance, or want of principle, its harmful results can be studied as one studies history, and personal conduct can be shaped more wisely in consequence.

Inherited failings are therefore the least excusable. Even the materialist, who regards them as products of physical structure, must admit that they can be corrected by appropriate training.

A healthy organism is capable of further development in any direction when suitable influences are intelligently applied. The defender of inherited failings can derive no real comfort from materialistic philosophy.

Failings peculiar to the individual are often more difficult to recognize. Those who possess them must rely, to some extent, on experience and on the warnings of others to gain the knowledge necessary for correction.

This should keep the thoughtful person open to instruction and ready to profit from the lessons life continually offers.

Self-reliance is a manly and admirable quality; self-sufficiency is unreasonable and therefore contemptible.

It is remarkable how few people grow genuinely wiser as the years advance.

The task of self-improvement is commonly postponed until some awakening experience forces it upon the judgment, and this often occurs only after the pliable years of youth have passed. By early adulthood, habits tend to harden, and failings become difficult to amend.

Much unhappiness and disappointment in later life could be avoided if the young were urged to begin the work of character training before it is fixed by circumstance, with inherited and acquired defects still uncorrected and errors of incomplete development left unaddressed.

Youth and adolescence offer the most hopeful period for cultivating the mind and shaping moral character with intelligence. No greater mistake can be made by a young and vigorous mind than to treat reason and moral judgment as faculties that will take care of themselves. The young person pays attention to physical development, trains the body, sharpens the senses, and congratulates himself on prudence when he seeks bodily health and strength.

Is it not folly of the gravest kind to neglect the systematic development of those higher powers in which human beings surpass all lower forms of life?

To care diligently for the body while neglecting the mind is the worst of failings—most disastrous in its consequences and least deserving of excuse.

End of the chapter

Chapter-2
Memory Its Limits Its Misuse and Its True Cultivation

This chapter shows that forgetfulness is often caused by wrong study methods, not by a weak mind. It teaches how proper understanding and organization can improve memory.

The power of remembering is not among the highest intellectual faculties. Many animals far below human beings in the scale of intelligence retain vivid recollections of places, persons, and events long after considerable time has passed. Even individuals of severely limited intellectual capacity are often observed to display what, in their condition, must be regarded as remarkable feats of memory. Yet the loss or serious weakening of this faculty produces grave mental disability, and when such impairment appears in a person who has previously shown no sign of defect, it naturally gives rise to uneasiness and a pressing desire to discover its cause.

Memory, in its ordinary and popular sense, is composed of two distinct powers: the power of fixing or retaining an idea in the mind, and the power of recalling it at will.

It is a familiar experience to feel certain that one knows a fact—the name of a person or place, the location of a misplaced object, or the date or sequence of an event—while being unable to bring it clearly into consciousness. Either of these powers may be at fault in what is commonly called "loss of memory." It is therefore of the greatest practical importance to determine which has failed, not only in the hope of remedying the defect, but also because such inquiry may reveal the true nature and origin of the trouble.

The fixing or retention of ideas is largely a matter of habit. Differences in the vividness and accuracy of original perception undoubtedly influence the strength of mental impressions. Some people receive ideas more slowly than others, while many who apprehend with great rapidity appear content to take up an idea momentarily and then let it slip away at once. Such persons do not truly make the idea their own or transform it into a mental possession; they grasp it as a porter lifts a package with which he has no concern, seizing it by whatever part is most convenient. Some learners acquire knowledge chiefly by the ear, catching the sound and rhythm of words rather than their meaning. Children who show an exceptional ability to memorize verses are often neither genuinely quick in understanding nor truly retentive.

Others learn mainly through the eye; anything that can be pictured, arranged in space, or placed within a definite form is readily appropriated.

Minds of this type are usually endowed with a keen sense of form and proportion. A third class depends on the habit of linking fragments of information together.

Such learners are perpetually piecing together a mental patchwork, retaining whatever can be attached to some existing fragment, while discarding what does not fit, however valuable it may be.

All these methods, and many others like them, represent peculiarities in the way impressions are received. As a rule, however, they do little more than lodge ideas in the outer chambers of the mind, where they are easily swept away by the first disturbance or displaced by the slightest internal commotion. When the memory suddenly appears blank, or seems to have shifted and lost its contents, and when there are no clear signs of disease, it becomes necessary to ask whether the event is not simply the clearing away of useless accumulation. This experience is by no means uncommon at the close of what is mistakenly called a completed "education."

Many young people, alarmed and distressed, are driven into needless anxiety, often encouraged by ill-informed advisers, with the fear that they are suffering from some grave and permanent defect. In reality, what has occurred is the sudden upsetting of a vessel overloaded with poorly arranged cargo. When such a craft rights itself, it is no real misfortune that the encumbrance has been thrown overboard, though it may be vexing to realize that there is no opportunity to return to port and reload with care. The practical course is to recover what is most useful from the floating wreck and stow it properly.

Breakdowns of this kind recur as long as the practice of cramming students for so-called competitive examinations continues to be admired. The idea of competitive testing, as commonly applied, has been socially and mentally harmful. Among its victims are not only the young men and women who experience the panic of mind to which reference has been made, but also the many overstrained and weakened intellects that are discarded as incapable by those who train and examine youth according to the fashions of the day. Some of the finest minds for genuine work are lost in this process.

When loss of memory occurs in this manner, especially soon after leaving school, after the completion of some severe mental effort, or at the moment when the mind is first confronted with the realities of practical life, there is no reason for extravagant alarm. The proper response is not to repeat the errors of a faulty system of training, but to repair the loss by developing the power of retention through steady and intelligent work in a new and healthier direction. In truth, a large proportion of alleged cases of "loss of memory" are simply the collapse of an unnatural method of education.

That the faculty of remembering itself appears weakened is not surprising. In addition to the immediate shock, there is the discovery that true power of retention was never developed at all. The genuine faculty of memory has not been cultivated, and the untrained mind must begin its education anew.

Only what has been thoroughly understood can be perfectly remembered. No method that fails to engage the natural powers of knowledge deserves the name of memory, or can truly perform its functions. The fixing of ideas in the mind depends chiefly on the way they are received and worked over in thought immediately after they are acquired. The power of recalling them, on the other hand, depends upon orderly arrangement and is therefore always capable of improvement.

Just as an orderly but forgetful person may place an object carefully in its proper position and later be unable to find it, so the mind may have stored an idea safely and completely and yet fail to recover it when required. It is often asserted that such failure must mean the idea was never properly stored. This may sometimes be true, but it is by no means a necessary conclusion. The fault is often as much in the method of searching as in the act of placing. Much depends upon how well a person knows his own mental possessions. If he is accustomed to revisit his knowledge, to review, examine, and refresh his ideas, he will usually be able to recover them readily when they are needed.

It may appear unscientific to employ such a comparison, for it is commonly assumed that ideas are recorded through combinations or alterations in the cells of the brain's cerebral tissue. Yet for practical minds, the notion of "placing" ideas and "finding" them again at will is more intelligible than technical terminology, and perhaps no less accurate in its essential meaning. The point to be clearly understood is this: inability to remember is as often a failure of method as a defect of power. Every person who suffers from forgetfulness should therefore exhaust all simpler and more comprehensible explanations before allowing anxiety to dwell on graver and less remediable causes. A few practical suggestions, drawn from observation and experience, may be helpful.

It is rarely useful to harass the memory during a moment of forgetfulness. When the right word does not immediately present itself, it is wiser to use another that will serve the purpose. Often the missing term will return by association; if it does not, the substitute will suffice. Forgetting a familiar name or expression is irritating, but the sense of annoyance and the mental disturbance it produces are unlikely to strengthen memory. On the contrary, they weaken it. A word or idea that refuses to answer the call of the will should be deliberately examined and thoughtfully learned when it is later recovered. In this way memory is strengthened. Struggling violently at the critical moment only increases the difficulty.

Equally harmful is reliance on so-called technical or artificial memories. When a large amount of material must be mastered quickly, the temptation to adopt mechanical formulas for facts or figures is strong. Yet this practice is destructive to the faculty of thought. It not only displaces genuine thinking, but weakens it. True retention is gained not by shortcuts, but by understanding.

The sure way to fix a subject in the mind is to master it thoroughly in all its aspects, so that both reason and judgment become familiar with it, each claiming what belongs to its own domain. Genuine knowledge implies that a subject has been brought clearly and in detail before the principal faculties of the mind, so that if one fails, another may supply the recall. Many people glance briefly at an object and then wonder why they cannot remember it. The faculties differ in their power of retention. In some minds, reason is the strongest instrument of memory. Such individuals remember chiefly what they have reasoned through, and if they forget something, they must recover it by reasoning, or it is lost.

Every thoughtful person should try to discover which faculty is most effective in his own mental economy and train it accordingly. Many who complain bitterly of poor memory possess excellent powers of recollection, but through ignorance or neglect they assign the task to the least competent faculty. They try to remember by sound when sight is their strongest aid, or they rely on the senses when their reasoning power is best fitted for the work. Memory is less a distinct faculty than a function, which may be carried out by one or several of the mind's powers, provided these are intelligently cultivated.

From this it follows that defects of memory are of many different kinds and must be carefully examined before drawing conclusions from partial impairment or even apparent failure. Some manifestations are striking. There may be an inability to recall events from a particular period of life, whether recent or remote. In the absence of clear brain disease, this form of loss is usually connected more closely with faulty apprehension than with recollection. What was least firmly grasped is most easily forgotten. In other cases, failure affects only certain classes of facts, such as dates or numbers, or even particular figures. Often this is associated with earlier excess—either undue strain in dealing with those subjects or a failure ever to master them thoroughly.

Some scientific explanations attribute these phenomena to the destruction of specific groups of brain cells. This may be so. Yet the fact that the blank is sometimes suddenly filled again, almost as if by an electric impulse, suggests that the impressions were not destroyed but temporarily withdrawn from active circulation, owing to some disturbance or diversion of nervous energy. Scientific theory readily allows this interpretation. Any condition that interferes with the flow of blood to the brain or disturbs the rhythm of nerve action may impair memory. For this reason, disorders of memory rightly command serious attention.

At the same time, it is important to dispel the harmful belief that every failure of memory is necessarily a sign of disease. It may simply be the result of defective training or mental overload. Nevertheless, early disturbance of memory is often one of the most significant warnings of brain strain. To test the symptom, one should search for possible bodily causes—anything that may have weakened the system or impoverished the blood. Loss of appetite, insufficient or improper nourishment, misuse of stimulants, excess of any kind followed by exhaustion, lack of sleep, prolonged physical or mental labor, or constitutional illness may all play a part. If such a cause is discovered, it should be removed without delay, and the effect carefully observed. When no lasting injury has been done, and the true source of trouble has been corrected, the brain usually returns to its normal condition, perhaps gradually, but clearly enough to show that the right course has been taken.

Most cases of memory failure are amenable to self-help. While medical intervention may sometimes be ineffective, and misguided treatment may even cause harm, the intelligent sufferer can often restore himself. The central principle of health and self-recovery may be expressed in a single word: order. Order is the universal law of natural life. It governs societies and must govern the individual. Measured by this standard, what is right, true, and worthy in conduct is easily distinguished from what is false, harmful, and degrading. Life itself, in its fullness, is orderly action. Every defect of life, every form of disease, and every failure of body or mind—including failure of memory—is the result of disorder. In its milder forms, defective memory arises from disorderly thinking; in its graver forms, it results from disordered nutrition and action of the brain.

End of the chapter

Chapter-3
Disordered Thinking and the Hidden Strain of the Mind

This chapter explains why thoughts sometimes become wild or restless. It shows how health, stress, and daily habits affect clear thinking. It also offers simple hope that the mind can recover with proper care and change.

Confusion of thought is a common human experience. Though familiar, it is often deeply distressing, and when it recurs frequently it gives rise to fears of lasting mental derangement. At times, thoughts seem to rush upon the mind like a pack of wolves, violent and uncontrollable, while consciousness stands alarmed and helpless, unable either to resist the assault or to restore order. In such moments the mental instrument—the organ through which we think—is weakened. This may occur through bodily illness affecting the mind, as in fever or other diseases accompanied by delirium; or through exhaustion following prolonged strain in a single direction, when the mind has been held too long upon anxiety, suspense, or perplexity. Similar confusion arises when the blood is impoverished and the brain is forced to work without sufficient nourishment, or when alcohol and other stimulants are abused, compelling the brain to consume in daily labor the reserves that nature intended for times of illness or emergency.

This violent and chaotic disorder of thought is almost always traceable to a physical cause and must be addressed through measures aimed at restoring general health. Sometimes relief follows a wise change in diet and the avoidance of beverages that give brief excitement only to be followed by collapse. A new arrangement of meals, a different but equally nourishing diet, or alterations in the amount of sleep—sometimes more, sometimes less—may bring improvement. Often, however, such measures are not enough. A complete change of scene and a thorough diversion of thought into new channels may be required. In nearly every case, there is some powerful though hidden cause, often unsuspected, that is undermining bodily vigor and, through it, mental strength.

There is another form of confusion which resembles this state but differs from it in essential character. Here the thoughts invade the mind not like ravening wolves, but like foolish sheep, tumbling over one another in dull disorder. The sensation is less terrifying than irritating, yet it is extraordinarily vexing, and if allowed to persist may prove as harmful in the end as the more violent disturbance. Sometimes this condition carries a touch of the grotesque, and its victim is mistaken for a wit. The humor, however, is uncertain and shallow. The flow of pleasantry suddenly breaks down, and a keen observer can detect the signs of conscious weakness and the inability to sustain the forced gaiety of an unnatural mental state.

When humor is absent, the confusion becomes simply harassing or distressing. The mind longs for rest, if only for a brief half-hour, or struggles to fix itself upon some subject—perhaps one of serious or even solemn importance—but cannot command attention. Those who suffer in this way may endure the condition for years, worn and harassed by a perpetual din of thoughts from which escape seems impossible. Like the rapid shifting of scenery seen from a speeding train, like the ceaseless rush of water or the swarming of bees, the disorder pursues them even into sleep. They do sleep, for otherwise life could not be sustained; yet the rest brings little comfort. They remain troubled or bewildered until consciousness fades, and they rise without refreshment, already weary and ill-prepared for the demands of another day.

This condition may be described as a disturbance of movement rather than of violence. In many cases it begins during bodily illness or becomes fixed through prolonged physical suffering, until it seems imprinted upon the brain itself. For a time—sometimes brief, sometimes long—the mind loses mastery over itself.

It becomes a mere mechanism for registering impressions without order or judgment, unable to distinguish clearly between images received through the senses and those that surge up from memory, as though a chaotic mental clearing were in progress and the whole household of thought were thrown into confusion. The power of deliberate thinking appears suspended, while consciousness stands by as a compelled witness, powerless either to restrain or rearrange the disorder.

The cure of this condition is often difficult and sometimes unattainable. The true cause must be removed, and this cause is frequently bound up with the individual's way of life, personal circumstances, or unavoidable obligations. To insist upon its removal may be as futile as commanding the tide to retreat. This is why many endure such confusion year after year, and why weaker minds may eventually succumb to unrelieved worry. Yet anything that breaks the monotonous rhythm of a life so consumed may open the way to recovery. At times, even severe domestic trials prove, in retrospect, to have been disguised blessings, providing the disruption needed for healing.

Pleasurable changes are, of course, the most desirable means of relief, as they work more swiftly and with less risk.

It is also noteworthy that minds suffering from this persistent confusion, though seemingly always on the verge of collapse, are not especially prone to be shattered by sudden shocks or great sorrows. Their danger lies not in catastrophe but in slow exhaustion from incessant worry. In other respects they are no weaker than the average intellect, and for this reason there is good ground for hope whenever proper treatment becomes possible.

Next in importance to the removal of the cause of this disturbed state of mind—and at times, though rarely, effective even without such removal—is the infusion of fresh vitality into the will. By a resolute act of judgment, the mind may in certain cases recover command over its own domain. This is a noble triumph of self-help, toward which all should strive, especially those who are unable to free themselves from the pressure of oppressive circumstances.

It is upon this effort that the intelligent mind should gather and concentrate its remaining strength. There exists in every part of human nature, mental and physical alike, a remarkable capacity for self-development, and every faculty grows through exercise. The effort that succeeds in restoring order, or even in keeping the rush of thoughts disentangled, if not fully disciplined, accomplishes more than a passing benefit. It reclaims a portion of the mental territory from the rebellious forces that threaten to perpetuate confusion within.

The most effective method is to engage the thinking faculty with some unfamiliar subject—how a thing is done, or the cause and explanation of a phenomenon previously unexplored. It is usually futile to attempt to cure confusion by a direct effort to suppress or control the thoughts themselves.

The sovereignty of the will can only be reasserted through the exercise of independent authority, first applied in a new sphere. Let the sufferer therefore choose a subject and mode of thought unlike any previously attempted. The desultory thinker may begin the study of mathematics, while one accustomed to figures may profit by immersing himself in history or fiction. Whatever the subject chosen, the exercise must be undertaken as a definite task. A fixed number of pages should be read or copied, whether interest is felt or not. Perseverance, and the renewal of effort at regular intervals—once or twice daily—imposed as a duty by the will and enforced by the same authority, generally bring success. When, in time, the power to follow a connected train of reasoning without irritation is restored, the gain is substantial.

The confusion under consideration may appear in many degrees, from occasional lapses of mental control arising in idle reverie, to a complete inability to do more than submit passively to thoughts that arrive unbidden and refuse dismissal. Two points must be clearly understood: first, that this condition is essentially a form of mental debility; and second, that it arises either from weakness of the controlling power or from the rebellion of those mental agents whose office it is to receive impressions and convey them to consciousness, thus placing the inner self in relation with the outer world.

When these agents escape discipline, they rush into consciousness laden with impressions of every kind—useful, harmful, and worthless alike—and heap them together without regard to will, order, or memory.

Other varieties of confused thinking could be described, but they all fall broadly within one or the other of the two classes already outlined.

The disturbance may be general, affecting thought in all its relations, or partial, confined to particular subjects. It may concern memories of past events, groups of names or numbers, or only those trains of reasoning that require deliberate thought.

These distinctions are of interest to the psychologist, but they are of little value to the sufferer, whose chief concern is relief rather than analysis. Excessive anxiety about subjective symptoms should be avoided. Although some temperaments find comfort in understanding an enemy, little is gained by brooding over the disorder itself. Far better to direct effort toward self-restoration.

Every known cause of weakness must be removed from daily habits, and in this task the will must take the lead. Regret is useless, and mere wishing is futile. Resolutions and intentions commonly lack force, and those born of fear are the least reliable of all. When the mind has been weakened by faulty self-management or by allowing trivial annoyances to overpower judgment, vows of reform are of little value. The simplest and least demonstrative methods of self-persuasion are the most effective. The future need not be anticipated, and the past, as far as possible, should be left behind.

Life is lived in the present, and self-recovery must begin now. It is precisely because the pain of wrong courses is immediate that reform is ever attempted.

The distress of being unable to command one's own thoughts should be sufficient to awaken a serious desire to recover the lost power of self-control.

To achieve this, the authority of the governing faculty of the mind must be promptly asserted. Questions such as these must be put by judgment to itself:

Why does this susceptibility or inclination rule me? Why do these troubles so deeply affect me? Why am I enslaved by a particular impulse?

When the honest answer follows—because the mind has not been fortified, or because inclinations have been allowed to dominate—the will must reassert its supremacy with the dignity proper to a faculty meant to command, not to obey.

Those who allow themselves to be wholly absorbed by circumstances, and who never rise above the immediate pressure of facts, are always liable to be crushed by the hardships of life. The path is roughest for those who walk it with eyes fixed only on its stones and obstacles.

It is bitter work forcing one's way through thorns without hope of rest or recompense beyond, and when the gaze is never lifted above the surrounding jungle, a person might as well grope through a forest where daylight never enters and the air is heavy with decay.

Those who find no comfort in life except what can be gathered from its darkest recesses are easy victims to gloomy and tormenting thoughts. Only a broader and higher view of the present and the future can bring relief.

Feelings do not grow dull under misfortune. On the contrary, the faculty of feeling becomes more irritable when it is constantly exercised upon petty annoyances, until sensibility itself grows morbid and the mind diseased.

The same law applies to impulses and appetites that are allowed to renounce obedience to judgment and will. Each act of rebellion strengthens the habit of revolt.

Soon the unrestrained instinct—whether vanity, love of pleasure, or any other—begins to usurp authority over the higher faculties it has displaced. In time it gains mastery over the mind itself, and the individual passes into insanity.

This is the painful and humiliating story of many a ruined life. The descent commonly begins with the indulgence of an unregulated ambition or a craving for self-gratification that has never been brought under discipline.

The indulgence is repeated, and, like a spoiled child, the desire—whatever its form—grows importunate.

Before long, judgment is no longer consulted. Next, the will loses its power to restrain.

Then, strengthened by its own rebellion, the insurgent impulse succeeds in bringing one faculty of the mind after another under its control, until all mental power becomes the servant of a single tyrant.

At last, the disordered forces either turn destructively upon one another or revolve helplessly around a single fixed idea.

To prevent such a catastrophe, there is but one effective remedy: the recovery of self-control. Confusion of thought is disorder, and the disordered activity of forces capable of the greatest good or the gravest harm can never be safe. The constant strain and misuse of the mental apparatus are self-destructive. Even the slightest impairment of the supreme authority of the will demands immediate and serious repair.

End of the chapter

Chapter-4
The Burden of Wakeful Thought and the Struggle for Rest

This chapter explains why thoughts seem stronger and more painful at night. It shows how lack of sleep can disturb judgment and increase fear. It teaches that peaceful rest is necessary for a healthy and stable mind.

The inability to quiet the rush of thoughts is often assumed to be the cause of sleeplessness, yet it is quite as likely that the inability to sleep throws the brain into a state of restless and anxious excitement. This latter explanation is often the more accurate, for the thoughts that distress or dominate the mind while it lies wakeful on the pillow are usually more vivid, more urgent, and more painful than those that occupy attention during the day. In part, this nocturnal exaggeration arises from the absence of external sights and sounds. The mind is thrown back upon itself and left to contend with its own reflections. Yet isolation alone does not fully explain the distorted intensity of thought that accompanies sleeplessness. During the day, even when the mind is absorbed in anxious reflection, it still retains the power to compare troubles with other experiences and to estimate losses and sorrows in some proportion. One of the most distressing features of wakeful thought at night is that the smallest anxieties swell into enormous proportions, so that matters which would cause little concern by daylight become sources of acute suffering in the darkness.

From these observations it may be concluded that what is commonly called sleeplessness from thought is a condition far more complex and unnatural than the phrase suggests. It is a state in which the brain seems to halt on the threshold of sleep. The mind, loosened from its anchorage to firm realities, is tossed to and fro, still occupied with the affairs of waking life, yet no longer able to judge their true bearing or proportion. This explains why habitual sufferers from sleeplessness often find it wise to rise and read when wakefulness persists. Reading not only induces drowsiness, but also prevents the mind from falling into that state of tumult which is so distressing and injurious in wakeful nights dominated by thought.

The loss of the ability to lay aside the burden of the day and to find rest in forgetfulness at night is among the most severe of personal afflictions. Only those who have endured it can fully appreciate how terrible it may become. When sleep is impossible, there is no escape, no respite, not even a momentary easing of the mental strain. The distress is heightened when, instead of relief, the mind enters a state in which every cause of anxiety is magnified. Sleeplessness of this kind is often the forerunner of insanity. It may be the earliest sign, or it may itself become the cause. The mental condition that arises when sleep is persistently resisted or denied is fundamentally unsound and tends toward disease.

Recognizing this danger, physicians often administer drugs to induce sleep. Their aim is twofold: to break the habit of wakefulness once it has formed, and to rescue the mind from a condition in which it is unsafe. This treatment would inspire greater confidence if it were certain that what is thus produced truly deserves the name of sleep. Unfortunately, there is little assurance of this. Sleep induced by drugs is often only a counterfeit state. If the mental disturbance is not relieved, the danger is merely concealed, not removed. It is true that some regain the ability to sleep naturally after a short course of sedatives. Such cases have undoubtedly been helped by something, though it remains open to question whether the benefit arose from the medicine itself or from mental influence. In any case, our chief concern lies with the state that precedes and obstructs sleep. We recognize its danger; the practical question is how it may be avoided.

When closely examined, the condition of thought that prevents sleep proves to be one in which the thinking faculty has escaped control. A subject may be introduced into the mind, but attention cannot be fixed, nor can thought be compelled to take a calm and comparative view. There is a marked tendency to exaggeration which judgment seems powerless to restrain. Alongside this there is another revealing feature: the impulse to repeat. The mind traverses the same ground again and again. The explanation is simple. There is a continual effort to sleep, and each train of thought breaks off at the very point where it should pass into a dream. Each renewal marks a fresh return to wakefulness.

Only careful observation of the inner experience reveals the true nature of this state. The mental faculties appear alert and intensely active, yet their exaggerated sensitivity is the result of arrested sleep. This condition mirrors what some experience when suddenly awakened. They recognize persons and surroundings, yet are seized by a sense of dread, almost of terror, while imagination distorts the scene in harmony with the confused mental state. That experience occurs during the slow return to wakefulness. The state we are describing arises on the path toward sleep, when progress is blocked. The important point is this: the distressing thoughts of the sleepless person are quite as likely to be the result of wakefulness as the cause of it.

Thoughts that pass through the mind as the brain drifts toward sleep should naturally slide into dream. They are transitional in character, vague and loosely defined, resembling the thoughts present during gradual awakening. The practical problem is to carry the mind across the boundary and transform conscious but uncontrollable thinking into dreaming. If this can be done naturally, without drugs that dull consciousness and mimic rather than produce sleep, the subject of thought soon changes and forgetfulness follows. There are two mental methods by which this transition may be attempted.

1. A thought or train of thoughts already present may be seized while it is still manageable and deliberately turned into something grotesque, thus preparing it to become the nucleus of an amusing dream. This method is easier to practice than to explain, yet experience shows it to be highly effective. Imagination must be gently directed to play with the thought and weave from it a slight and fanciful scene. Only a small effort is needed to preserve the connection; too much control will defeat the purpose by restoring full wakefulness. The essence of the method lies in holding the thought steady while projecting it into a dreamlike sequence. This process is natural and harmless, unlike the artificial stupefaction produced by drugs, which overpower rather than soothe the mind.
2. The second method consists in giving the mind a monotonous task, such as counting or repeating simple actions. This approach, though commonly recommended, is often less effective in severe cases of sleeplessness from thought than the former method. A mind harassed by anxiety resists being diverted into empty exercises. Imagining cornfields, rising tides, or drifting clouds of smoke may sometimes succeed, but it is not always possible to exclude troubling thoughts and fix attention on such neutral images. To do so often requires an effort as great as that which has already failed. For the wakeful and worried, it is generally easier to transform an existing troubling thought into harmless imagery than to introduce a wholly new and unrelated idea.

It may be worthwhile to attempt the familiar method of connecting and monotonous imagining, but when this fails, as it often does, recourse should be had to the artifice already described. As a rule, it will be found effective, although at first, when the mind is oppressed by gloomy reflections or forebodings, the effort to think grotesquely may feel harsh and even offensive. For example, a person troubled by distressing circumstances and fearing financial ruin should compel the mind to pursue the thought until the comic side of reversal becomes visible.

He may follow the imagined path of his supposed decline, the new mode of life to which he might be driven, the curious acquaintances he may form, the unexpected scenes he might witness, and the remarkable places he could be led to visit. All considerations of probability must be set aside, and the mind allowed, or rather compelled, to work out the idea freely. At first the effort will be laborious and uncongenial, but unless the mind is entirely devoid of humor, the strain will gradually relax, and with the sense of relief sleep will come.

As has been shown, sleeplessness from thought is often not the cause but the consequence of wakefulness induced by physical conditions. It is just as easy to push exertion beyond the point at which natural sleep offers relief as it is to fall short of the measure of activity needed to promote rest.

Most persons who suffer from persistent wakefulness are not idle, but overactive.

They labor hard and exhaust themselves, though often in an ill-directed manner. Some dissipate their strength in the pursuit of pleasure; others are so absorbed in work that they cannot lay aside its claims when the time for rest arrives.

Perhaps the most common cause of this form of sleeplessness is the habit of carrying unfinished work from day to day, instead of dividing it in such a way that natural pauses occur, allowing the mind to rest with the consciousness that duty has been fulfilled and a task completed. Nothing so readily invites sleep as the feeling of contentment, and this feeling can generally be secured by assigning oneself in the morning a definite amount of work that can be finished before night. When the obligation has been discharged, the mind seeks and usually finds repose as the reward of its effort.

To break off suddenly in the midst of labor and then expect sleep to obey at once is unreasonable. Though body and mind are closely linked, it is rarely possible to command the physical organism to sleep instantly at will.

Regularity is essential to healthy action, not merely punctuality in hours, but the steady habit of completing the day's work within the time appointed for it.

A common error is to plan the work of the following day at night. This is like turning a new page when the book should be closed and laid aside. The proper time for planning is the morning. If this duty were then performed, many restless dreams and much of the feeling of having passed a whole night in disturbed thinking would be avoided.

The weariness of reluctant waking, when no immediate purpose presents itself to the mind, often nullifies the benefit of sleep. When a person begins to toss restlessly, it is often wiser to rise; or, if that is not possible, to occupy the mind in calmly arranging the tasks of the coming day. Each night should close the book of life with the sense that accounts have been fairly settled. The business of the morning is to carry forward what remains and to begin anew.

No prudent person will risk the danger of carrying unresolved balances into the hours of sleep. There are many reasons, both physical and mental, why the day's reckoning should not be made at night, but one is sufficient. To sleep upon resolutions for self-improvement is a mistake. During sleep the force of motive subsides, and the purpose formed at night is often weakened or forgotten by morning. It is far better to complete the work of the day, close the record, and seek rest. When consciousness returns, the situation may be reviewed, plans for the future laid, and, while the impression is fresh, action taken.

We are too prone to moralize at night, and then to resume the routine of life, forgetting both the lessons learned and the resolutions formed, after the lapse of memory which even light sleep brings. Sleeping and waking are mutually dependent states and must follow one another in orderly succession if health is to be maintained. Life itself moves by rhythm, and a sound mind in a sound body can be preserved only through harmony, method, and orderly self-control exercised by the will.

End of the chapter

Chapter-5
When Speech Falters and Thought Loses Its Discipline

This chapter explains how thinking and speaking are closely connected. It shows how careless thoughts can lead to hesitation in speech. It teaches that clear and disciplined thinking improves clear speaking.

Speech, in a practical sense, is more than a mere instrument for expressing thought. It is so closely bound up with the act of thinking that little beyond the simplest recognition of sensory impressions can occur without the aid of language, at least in some elementary form. Thought and speech are inseparable. Speech need not be articulate or audible; it may exist on any level, from spoken words to the silent mental rehearsal of sounds, as when a person thinks of a word and distinctly apprehends its pronunciation without uttering it aloud. Careful observation of this inward act of pronouncing words in thought reveals a restrained impulse to move the lips and tongue, an impulse usually held in check so that no visible muscular movement occurs. Yet exceptions to this restraint not only confirm the rule but also demonstrate how intimately thought and bodily action are connected.

During sleep and dreaming, and in certain waking states—especially among the aged or those of weakened intellect—the lips may move with almost every thought, though no sound is produced. When the normal restraint is weakened, or the impulse unusually strong, thoughts may escape into speech without intention. Many amusing anecdotes attest how individuals have betrayed their true feelings by unconsciously speaking their thoughts aloud. Faults in speech, therefore, often arise from defects in thought, since the two functions depend upon each other; or, conversely, errors of speech may react injuriously upon the mind. It is of real importance to determine the true cause of hesitation or error in speech in any given case.

The first step is to make sure that the difficulty does not arise from ordinary confusion of thought, caused by careless habits of thinking or the pernicious practice of allowing thoughts to drift aimlessly. Many people permit their minds to become overgrown with tangled mental undergrowth, so that only the most agile powers of attention can carry a thought safely through. They then complain of difficulty in directing thought, when the true fault lies in neglect. Clear away the mental jungle, and thought will no longer be forced to wander by indirect paths, often to be lost altogether. The only remedy here is cultivation. The amount of labor required will vary. For some, it resembles the toil of clearing raw land before it can be made productive; for others, simple weeding and loosening of the soil will suffice. In every case, however, the work must be done. A mind left weedy, confused, and uneven cannot be expected to speak clearly or accurately. Excluding defects of the physical mechanism of speech, it may be safely asserted that neglect of self-control in thinking is the most frequent and, in many ways, the most harmful cause of hesitation and error in speech.

When a person who has previously spoken with ease and fluency begins to hesitate, there is usually cause for concern. If general health appears sound, and no obvious emotional shock or nervous strain has occurred, there is likely some physical or mental disturbance operating unseen. If the cause is physical, attempts at speech are often accompanied by trembling or twitching of the lips, mouth, jaw, or neighboring muscles. Should such signs be noticed by others, or perceived by the individual himself, medical advice should be sought without delay. These symptoms may arise from conditions that range from trivial weakness to serious disease, and only skilled judgment can distinguish between them.

More commonly, however, hesitation is mental in origin. Either the mind is overcrowded with thoughts and unable to command the function of finding words, or that function has been so weakened that it cannot respond to the authority of the will. It reacts quickly to intrusive influences that have no rightful claim, yet when judgment issues a command, it fails to obey. This condition results from undisciplined and disorderly habits of thought. The mental exhaustion produced by such dissipation, regardless of the direction in which thoughts are allowed to wander, is among the most dangerous states into which an otherwise healthy brain can fall. Long before any outward sign is visible, the mind itself is conscious of the peril. Hesitation in speech is often the first external indication, but by the time it appears, the weakening influence has usually been at work long enough to do serious harm. It is not yet too late to recover, but the danger is real and grave.

On this point, plain speaking is necessary. Habits of brooding, idle musing, or indulging in vivid mental scenes in which one imagines oneself an actor, gradually enlisting imagination and even sensation, are among the most frequent, though least acknowledged, causes of mental collapse. It may seem harsh to say so, yet a large proportion of those, especially among the young and middle-aged, who spend long years in asylums with broken minds, have contributed to their own ruin. Any one of many circumstances may precipitate the final breakdown or shape its outward form, but the predisposing cause that makes such disaster possible is the habit of allowing thought to roam unchecked—first harmlessly, then along forbidden paths, and finally wherever the darker impulses of one's nature may lead.

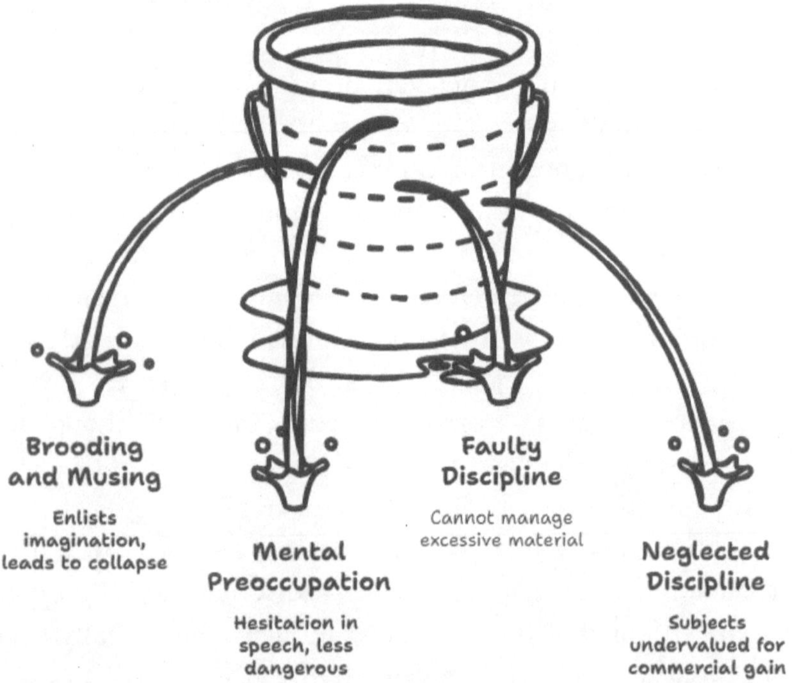

The habit of mental preoccupation, which sometimes reveals itself through hesitation in speech, is less dangerous than outright weakness, yet it should not be ignored. Having too much to think about is less harmful than losing the power of voluntary thought altogether, but it remains an evil. Often "too much" does not mean an excessive quantity of material, but more than can be managed under faulty discipline. The same burden might be borne easily if thinking were properly ordered.

Modern education increasingly neglects this discipline. Subjects once valued for their power to train and strengthen the mind are being set aside because they do not yield immediate commercial advantage. Greek, Latin, mathematics, and similar studies are undervalued precisely because they do not readily translate into marketable returns. Yet it is these very disciplines that once furnished the mind with habits of order, control, and endurance, without which both thought and speech inevitably suffer.

We are already beginning to reap the consequences of this time-serving policy in education, and they appear in the widespread breakdown of young minds when confronted with duties that require the handling of many thoughts at once. The untrained and disorderly thinker cannot readily choose words. He has "no time" to arrange them and often cannot find them when they are needed. He is, as he excuses himself, "thinking of something else." It has even come to be regarded as a mark of cleverness to be "abstracted," "deeply engrossed," or "overwhelmed with things to think about." These are the pitiable apologies of a generation of confused and incompetent thinkers whose speech betrays their condition. A skillful talker will sometimes bridge the gap between two suitable words rather than insert a wrong one. The ingenuity with which this is accomplished by self-possessed yet confused speakers may amuse the observer, but the underlying disorder of thought remains, thinly veiled by clever artifice.

When increasing hesitation in speech is not the result of serious mental weakness—and the person affected is usually privately aware of the cause—the remedy lies in adopting a better method of thinking. The first effort must be toward greater calmness, the second toward greater order. There is in thinking a process equivalent to punctuating a written page or fastening a thread securely in needlework. When this process is neglected, as it often is by those miscalled rapid thinkers—who are in truth careless or impetuous—confusion inevitably follows, and it manifests itself in hesitation and error of speech.

Verbal mistakes usually arise from confusion of thought, though they may also be caused by disease. It is important to distinguish between these two sources.

When errors occur irregularly, without a consistent pattern, and wrong words appear to intrude at random—perhaps drawn from another idea passing through the mind at the same moment—the confusion may safely be attributed to faulty mental discipline and treated accordingly. If, however, particular words once familiar are persistently forgotten, certain numbers disappear from memory, or errors follow a definite pattern in speaking or writing, the condition may be more serious and professional advice should be sought. One striking feature of early speech disorders arising from physical causes, such as the beginnings of brain disease, is that specific elements of knowledge seem to be erased, and particular forms of reasoning become impossible, while the general capacity for mental work remains largely intact.

Much suffering could be avoided if, in all forms of mental disturbance not directly due to brain disease, those who feel something amiss within themselves—and such premonitions of disorder are more common than is admitted—would take the initiative in correcting the fault by submitting the mind to regular training. Whether the sensation is one of irritability or dull pressure, the wiser course is self-discipline.

A practical method is to assign the mind a daily task of reading, not too long, but sufficiently demanding to occupy the thoughts fully. This should be done at fixed hours. Regularity is essential, as the object is to restore mental rhythm and strengthen attention. In cases where hesitation and speech errors indicate impaired vigor of mind, much benefit may be gained by reading aloud daily for an hour or more to family members.

Reading aloud when alone is not only useless but potentially harmful. The mind then invents an imaginary audience, and this habit of mental fabrication is one of the shortest and most dangerous paths toward serious mental disorder, especially for those with vivid imaginations. Another danger lies in the mind's attention being drawn to the sound of its own voice, which may encourage further confusion. It is through this gradual substitution of imagined voices for real ones that some weak or morbid minds come to believe they are receiving supernatural communications, when in reality they are merely hearing echoes of their own thoughts.

When reading aloud to others from a healthy and engaging book, the strained connection between thought and speech is eased. Used wisely, this practice is among the most effective remedies for disorders of speech. Success depends upon choosing material that genuinely interests the reader and is challenging enough to command attention. In some cases, the exercise becomes even more beneficial when one reads aloud in one language from a text written in another, such as reading a French work to an English audience. This practice strengthens both memory and word selection, precisely the faculties most in need of cultivation.

Hesitation and errors in speech are never trivial. In their milder forms they call for serious and determined self-improvement; in their graver manifestations they warn of dangers threatening both brain and mind.

End of the chapter

Chapter-6
Low Spirits as a Disorder of Mind and Vitality

This chapter explains that lasting low spirits often come from exhaustion, not from simple sadness.It shows why wrong treatment and quick excitement can make the condition worse. It teaches that careful timing, healthy habits, and self-control are the safest path to recovery.

Everyday life offers ample material to dampen feeling and rob the mind of its natural buoyancy, without the added burden of persistent low spirits as a settled mental condition. Yet this state so often assumes the character of a truly morbid affection, attacks individuals not naturally inclined to despondency, and reveals such close connections with bodily health, that it must be recognized as a form of disease. Constitutional melancholy, which marks certain temperaments, is not so much depression as a life lived in a lower emotional key. Within this narrower range, such individuals experience variations of mood as real and significant as those whose temperament is pitched higher and who therefore appear capable of greater exhilaration.

It is of the first importance to determine whether the person under observation is not naturally marked by this quieter and more restrained tone of feeling. Unhealthy mental states are usually detected by contrast with what has gone before. The lively and excitable may become fixed and unresponsive, the self-controlled irritable, the calm suddenly passionate. It is the change that calls for attention. When low spirits afflict a mind previously marked by resilience and cheerfulness, there must be a cause, and prudence demands watchfulness. Well-meaning efforts to stimulate emotions that are no longer under control may unintentionally do harm.

Few errors are more common than the assumption that low spirits can be relieved by direct appeal to the sufferer. Even intelligent and experienced people, who deal skilfully with other mental disturbances, often fail in their attempts to alleviate melancholy. They entreat, argue, exhort, or even rebuke, urging the sufferer to rouse himself, to take interest in life, to abandon brooding thoughts. Such methods might succeed if the trouble lay lightly on the surface. But the condition here described is far deeper. It is a chilling of all energies, a blight that drains vitality, a poison that weakens and paralyzes the whole system.

While the depression lasts, it is useless to search the consciousness for its cause. One might as well look for the weapon that struck a man senseless while he lies faint and bleeding, in need of immediate help. Even if the cause were discovered at such a moment, nothing could be done to prevent further harm. If the low spirits are the result of error or mismanagement of self, the time when the crushed spirit is enduring the penalty is the worst moment for reproach. Reasoning is futile when self-control is at its weakest. Judgment and will lie dormant. The stirrings of conscience during depression are largely emotional, and the resolutions formed are barren. Tears of regret and efforts at resolve in this state are worse than useless; they resemble the struggles of one sinking in quicksand, which only hasten the descent.

The phase of mental collapse must be allowed to pass. Here, however, lies the difficulty. When reaction begins and the cloud slightly lifts, interference may already be too late. The mind has entered another stage, no less unhealthy than the depression that preceded it. There is no fixed sign that marks the precise moment for helpful intervention. The wisest course is to watch the changes of temperament closely and, guided more by time than by symptoms, to present a new and engaging interest—a journey, an undertaking, a congenial task—just before recovery begins. The mind is brooding, on the verge of waking. Only familiarity with the rhythm of previous attacks can indicate the moment. Whatever most strongly engages the awakening faculties is likely to hold them for a time. The struggle then is between healthy and morbid influences. If genuine help is sought, the right means must be chosen, and the wrong ones—preaching, moralizing, exhorting, and rallying—carefully avoided. When thought revives and the faculties rebound, they must be occupied with cheerful and wholesome subjects.

It is a serious mistake to assume that good has been achieved merely because a melancholic patient has been roused.

The apparent brightness of such intervals is often more dangerous than the period of exhaustion and gloom. When the mind becomes active again, it frequently resumes the work of self-injury. The gravest harm is done in these so-called lucid intervals. Unless consciousness is absorbed in healthy activity, it will return to the morbid processes that end in renewed depression. The true task is to prevent the next collapse. This can be accomplished only by removing the unhealthy excitement that usually precedes it. Healthy activity promotes sound nutrition and restores strength to both mind and body. Any form of activity that fails to improve the quality of the organ engaged weakens it and tends to distort normal function.

The persistent morbid state known as melancholy is gradually built up through repeated attacks of depression and despondency. It is during the intervals of apparent relief, while this destructive process is advancing, that the cause may be discovered and, in many cases, removed. The sufferer is often aware of how the depression has arisen, or of the train of thought by which it has been introduced; yet it is useless, and indeed a mistake, to attempt to draw out this knowledge by questioning. Any known cause will usually be denied. Unless the individual becomes, in some measure, his own physician, there is little hope of direct cure.

The state of mind commonly fluctuates with the condition of the body. When energy is exhausted, the natural flow of vitality is checked. Depression frequently springs from a physical cause, and if it were rightly understood and wisely treated, little harm would result. Unfortunately, serious misunderstanding prevails. It has been discovered that by means of stimulants, the reserve of nervous force—which nature has provided not merely for emergencies, but as the foundation of enduring vitality—can be forced into service for the passing moment. This reserve may be likened to the stored air that gives power to a bagpipe. Careless of the ruinous cost of this expedient, stimulants are resorted to, and the excitement they produce is mistaken for healthy action. The exhausted brains, irritable nervous systems, impaired intellects, incapacity for useful work, and the blighted lives of those who have relied upon this pernicious palliative should serve as a warning both to sufferers tempted to try it and to friends seeking a remedy.

Lowness of spirits is exhaustion. Anything that consumes the remaining reserve of strength must ultimately aggravate the very condition it is intended to relieve.

By stimulating instead of nourishing the brain, the mind is gradually reduced to lasting inefficiency, whereas, if left to recover without such misguided interference, it would likely regain its natural buoyancy. There is always danger in converting a temporary suspension of function, due to recoverable weakness, into permanent incapacity by applying excitement while power is still failing. This danger is especially grave in relation to the functions of the brain.

It is therefore an act of plain prudence to treat low spirits as a state of temporary exhaustion and to allow time for restoration through proper nutrition of the brain. If a person is conscious of having passed through a cycle of elation followed by depression, he should avoid the cause, whatever it may have been.

It is always a miserable, and generally a ruinous, bargain when judgment is degraded enough to exchange mental strength and sanity for transient pleasure.

The wise will refuse such a barter. The particular form of dissipation matters little, except that some indulgences ruin body and mind together. All forms of unnatural, ill-timed, or excessive excitement act in the same destructive way, weakening vitality and ultimately destroying it.

Few conditions are so widely lamented and so poorly understood as this one. Men and women may endure long lives of sorrow, hardship, and heartache without suffering from this malady. In such cases, the depression they feel arises from pressure and burden rather than from exhaustion.

When hope appears, however faint, the mind makes an immediate effort to rise. The elasticity of healthy spirits is remarkable, and their power of recovery when relief comes is often astonishing. By contrast, the loss of resilience that follows repeated exhaustion deepens with each recurrence. The true nature of this lowness will never be understood unless it is recognized as what it really is.

Those who study mental disease describe a condition known as rotary mania, in which periods of excitement alternate with phases of melancholy.

This is merely an intensified form of the state under discussion. Periodic attacks of low spirits, whatever name is given to them, are morbid manifestations of the same order, differing only in degree and not yet fully developed.

Those who suffer from this affliction should be on their guard. Above all, they must recognize its nature and foresee its possible outcome.

They should also understand how largely the prevention of the disorder, in its earliest stages, lies within their own power of self-help.

Once the condition has passed beyond this point, assistance from others becomes necessary. If those who would help reflect carefully on the principles outlined here, they may avoid doing harm and perhaps render lasting service.

Two extremes must be avoided with equal care: doing too much and doing too little.

Harmful interference is a serious error, but standing by idly while individuals drift into hopeless melancholy or mental decay is a greater one. Exceptional patience and sound judgment are required to decide when and how to intervene. The right moment must be determined by the stage of the attack rather than by isolated symptoms. The aim should be to guide the mind back to health along new paths, awakening fresh interests and calling forth new impulses.

The two most fatal dangers to be avoided are despondency and quackery. There is always hope in faithful obedience to the laws of nature, and despair in special and artificial treatments, however cleverly devised.

End of the chapter

Chapter-7
Temperament Its Nature Its Disorders and Its Meaning

This chapter explains the different kinds of bad temper and their causes. It shows how physical weakness or unused energy can lead to anger. It teaches that balance, work, and self-control help build a calm and stable character.

Bad temper—or, more accurately, lack of true temper—is among the most regrettable and serious defects of character. The explosive irritability that causes a person to "boil over," as the common phrase has it, at the slightest provocation is not, however, the gravest form of this fault. It bears much the same relation to genuine malignity as nervous excitability does to cowardice. A person who starts at a sudden noise may yet face real danger with steadiness and courage; startled by an unexplained sound or shadow, he may nevertheless remain firm and resolute when confronted with a known threat.

In the same way, those who are superficially excitable are often among the most self-controlled and composed once the first outburst of feeling has, as it were, cleared the air. Such temperaments may not promote the easiest domestic or social relations, yet they are far more compatible with the demands of sincere friendship than many placid and inscrutable dispositions that are difficult to read and harder to trust. Temper of mind and character may be compared to the tension of strings in a musical instrument, or to the tempering of steel. When the strain is evenly adjusted, the tones produced are true, and the strength reliable. When there are defects in quality or balance, the vibration is false and the strength deceptive. Temper, in short, is the outcome of personal constitution, in which the individual qualities of mind and body, and their mutual interaction, play a decisive role. A full scientific treatment would require consideration of far more mental and physical elements than can be embraced here. For present purposes, it is enough to glance at a few of its practical aspects.

The emotional side of human nature lies near the surface and responds readily to impressions that are themselves superficial. This is why feeling, in its ordinary sense, is no reliable measure of deeper sympathy or genuine benevolence. Emotional display may be abundant where true kindness is scant. The surface may be stirred by every passing breeze while the depths remain stagnant. Conversely, a deep and steady current of feeling may impart such strength to the whole that the surface appears comparatively unmoved, just as a leaf may ripple a still pool, while a stone cast into a swift stream scarcely disturbs it.

The history of crime offers painful illustrations of the worthlessness of emotional display as a moral test. Some of the most cruel and calculating crimes have been committed by men and women of highly emotional and sentimental natures, capable of intense feeling and rapid emotional response. Certain notorious poisoners, for example, have exhibited almost excessive sensibility. Nothing, therefore, can be safely inferred about moral worth from mere emotional mobility. Yet in a sound and well-balanced nature there should be harmony between surface feeling and deeper character, and when the psychophysical constitution is healthy and well tempered, such harmony is usually present.

Tempers are called "good" or "bad" according to the degree of unity they maintain among the various qualities of mind and body. Too often temper is judged by isolated peculiarities rather than by the general character of which it is only one expression. If temper consistently mirrored character, such rough judgment might be excusable; but this is seldom the case.

Most people are shaped and modified by circumstances and associations, and the result is more often a mixed than a homogeneous character. Without such homogeneity, an even and reliable temper is impossible.

Hasty tempers usually spring from irritability that lies close to the surface. This fault is commonly due to lack of harmony between mind and body, one being weaker than the other.

Physical weakness often produces irritability because the body cannot promptly and adequately carry out the demands of the mind. There is perhaps no clearer evidence that the brain is an instrument rather than the source of mind than the impatience with which the will rebels against its own physical limitations. Consider the irritability born of humiliation and vexation at being unable to meet the ordinary trials of life with greater calm—a frequent and poorly understood cause of ill temper. What is this but a mind chafing against the weakness of its own bodily instrument? The person is irritable because he is irritable; cause and effect become confused, and consciousness is entangled in its own distress.

Those who suffer chronic pain or prolonged mental anxiety know by bitter experience how severe this form of irritability can be, and how little sympathy it usually receives. Particularly distressing is the self-consciousness of those who appear outwardly healthy yet possess fragile constitutions or endure hidden suffering. The effort to remain calm, to exercise self-control, to resist petty irritations, and to present a brave front to circumstances becomes exhausting. Strength is wasted, and matters grow worse instead of better. It may bring some comfort to such sufferers to know that their condition is recognized and that its roots lie largely in bodily causes, even though the distress is experienced in the mind.

Those who are weak or limited in mental power, by contrast, often suffer less themselves from irascible tempers than they inflict upon others. Full-blooded and passionate individuals usually possess more energy than they know how to govern. This surplus force demands an outlet, and provided it can be released harmlessly, the outburst, though unpleasant, is not necessarily a grave evil. Vigorous constitutions confined by disease or disability are especially prone to such explosions.

Among prisoners this condition often appears as a recurring disorder and is frequently misunderstood. Instead of being treated as a form of explosive disease, it is too often punished as deliberate misconduct or rebellion, thereby increasing suffering rather than relieving it.

The remedy for this last-mentioned form of temper—whether it arises from a mind that is healthy but limited, or from one that is morbid or unoccupied, which in effect amounts to much the same—must be sought in work. Physical force requires employment, and it is best when it can be directed toward some useful purpose with tangible results. If those fiery and impassioned individuals of every age and condition, who rage through life like untamed creatures to the discomfort of all around them, could be provided with suitable occupation and a wholesome outlet for their energy in productive labor, they would be spared much remorse, and others much needless irritation and harm. The self-cure of this temperament should consist in exercise of sufficient amount and appropriate kind to engage the body fully and give the mind firmer control over the organism for which it is responsible.

The opposite temperament—the cold, sullen, and seemingly unimpressionable—deserves far greater caution and concern. There exists a certain stolid disposition, allied to dullness, which can be judged only in relation to the character as a whole. It may result from general inertness, or from an absence of quick sensibility beneath which lurk the vices of mere animalism. When, however, a rigid and immovable exterior conceals signs of keen intelligence, appearances become suspect, and reserve invites mistrust. It would be unjust to assert this universally, yet it is generally true that such mysterious temperaments are dangerous. The moral nature appears hardened. The inner self—the heart, however named—stands in unnatural isolation from the outer world. True companionship becomes difficult, and confidence, unless earned through long observation of conduct, is almost impossible. The temper may be stable, yet it is not trusted, because it lies beyond ordinary social tests and offers none of the familiar signs by which character is commonly read. It resembles a barometer with its face covered: the instrument may respond accurately to changes in the atmosphere, but no one can tell whether it does or not. The individual becomes a moral enigma.

When this immovable temperament is joined to a kindly and upright nature, the person is at first viewed with suspicion, even dislike. If, in time, he is understood, he may be respected, but he is rarely loved. There can be little doubt that such a frigid and unresponsive exterior, coupled with an unimpassioned character, is a misfortune. Those who feel themselves cut off from others by a lack of ordinary emotional responsiveness would do well to cultivate feeling at least to the extent of gaining command over expression. It is a genuine loss to be so reserved that trust cannot be inspired, even when the real disposition is generous and benevolent.

In some cases this reserve is assumed rather than innate. Acute sensibility may be deliberately suppressed after observing emotional display that is insincere or at odds with character in others. The observer represses his own feelings, and over time they become fixed and unyielding. Similar effects may arise from prolonged association with uncongenial or false natures. A person who appears cold and unfeeling may have withdrawn into himself for self-protection, or under the influence of strong aversion, and thus becomes outwardly immobile though inwardly sensitive. In studying individual character, all these possibilities must be weighed. The task is complex and delicate, and misunderstandings are therefore common. Many of the tempers and characters we encounter are not native growths, but the products of misinterpretation and circumstance. A sincere and resolute mind will strive against such influences and dismantle the barriers accident has erected around it. Through this corrective effort, faults of temper may be softened and false impressions dispelled.

The genuinely sullen temperament, however, is scarcely amenable to any treatment aimed merely at altering outward manner. It is almost invariably the reflection of an unsympathetic nature, selfishly absorbed in its own hidden purposes. The isolation visible at the surface mirrors an isolation of the heart. Appeals from without evoke no response because they are not felt. There is no expression of feeling because there is none to express. Consciousness is absorbed in private concerns and remains unmoved by the needs, sorrows, or joys of others. When such a temper is allied with intelligence, it indicates a deep-rooted selfishness of the lowest kind, beyond the reach of superficial reform. The motives may not be actively malicious, yet they stand in no vital relation to the surrounding world and acknowledge no responsibility to human suffering or sympathy.

It would be unjust to say that society lays excessive emphasis on peculiarities of temper, but it must be admitted that the prevailing mode of judgment is unsound. Temperamental traits are not directly subject to the will, and it is well that they are not. Attempts to reform temper by direct attack are therefore usually futile. The wiser aim is to correct the defects of inner character from which outward faults arise. Irritability should be addressed through care of physical health and by avoiding habits of thought that leave the mind exposed to chance or enslaved by circumstance. For most people, deliberate cultivation of emotional excitability is a mistake. The conventional encouragement of taste—especially dramatic taste, to which highly sensitive natures are prone—often fosters sentimentality. Unless the heart is as deep as the feelings are quick, the outer temperament soon ceases to reflect inner truth. When emotion no longer expresses genuine sentiment, irritability and insincerity soon follow.True temper, in its only worthy sense, rests upon sincerity and consistency. If the heart is right, temper may be improved by gaining fuller command over the emotional life, but improvement must begin within and work outward. To cleanse only the exterior while the interior remains corrupt is not reform but deception. Such artificial calm is more harmful than the wildest outbursts of an uncontrolled nature. Temper is a quality of order and self-government, and to be genuine it must spring naturally from an orderly and disciplined character. Otherwise it is not temper at all, but a counterfeit—worse than worthless because it is false and encourages insincerity.Strong and deep feeling naturally seeks warm expression in earnest speech and vigorous action. The grace that self-restraint lends to character is admirable only when passion is governed by reason, not merely suppressed by policy or chilled by calculating self-interest. The novelist often portrays the consummate villain as perfectly controlled and the innocent hero as impulsive and emotionally generous. Though the device is overused and exaggerated, it reflects a truth of human nature.The highest ideal of humanity presents perfect sincerity as its foremost excellence, and faithful expression of inner character completes the picture. The moment consistency is broken—whether by excessive display of feeling or by artificial restraint—harmony is lost, and with it every claim to respect grounded in integrity.

End of the chapter

Chapter-8
Mental Languor and the Loss of Intellectual Vitality

It warns against forcing the mind through sheer willpower or relying on stimulants, both of which may do harm. Instead, it recommends rest, variety of activity, exercise, proper nourishment, and adherence to sound habits of living. When wisely managed, mental languor need not become serious; but if ignored and resisted imprudently, it may be an early sign of deeper breakdown.

There is a form of mental disturbance to which scholars and students are especially prone. It often comes without warning and at once weakens the very springs of effort. Ambitions that once seemed attainable now appear beyond reach; the prizes of life lose their attraction; the long-desired fruit tastes sour, and the game seems hardly worth the cost of playing. Many distinguished writers have described such experiences.

It is not quite the same as depression or low spirits, nor is it true exhaustion or overstrain. Rather, it is a condition of mental languor or lethargy. Everything becomes an effort. Stimuli that once called the faculties into ready action lose their power. The will to work seems to have vanished.

This state of mind, as noted, is one to which studious people are particularly liable. A thoughtful observer once described it as the scholar's special affliction, bred beneath a brow that labors intensely but sweats little. Though it may pass quickly, it is apt to recur. The editor at his desk suddenly feels its fatal influence steal upon him. His hold on the subject slackens, the pen slips from his hand, ideas move sluggishly or escape altogether, and he finds himself utterly blocked, unable to proceed.

The lawyer, listening to a client, becomes aware that he is no longer following the narrative. His mind refuses to grasp and apply the principles of law. Thoughts grow hazy and disconnected. He fears he may yawn openly and feels an aversion to the entire affair, desiring only to dismiss the visitor without revealing his mental inertia.

So it is with the college student preparing eagerly for examination. At the very moment when double effort is required, an irresistible inclination seizes him to lean back, throw aside his books, and allow his thoughts to wander aimlessly over trivial matters. Even the power to resist this seductive influence is lacking. The inspiring music of the future, which usually stirs him to action, sounds distant and faint. Instead, a subtle and enervating whisper steals over the mind, inviting rest and abandonment of effort.

This condition is especially common in youth. With some, it recurs at certain hours of the day; with others, at particular seasons of the year. In some it is mild and occasional; in others it becomes serious, impairing usefulness and still more deeply affecting happiness. It often afflicts earnest and conscientious workers—men of real ability, great diligence, and high ambition. To them it brings not only loss of time but painful self-distrust. They reproach themselves with inefficiency, mistake this peculiar state for indolence, and accuse themselves of laziness. Such reflections follow them even into their more active hours and cast a shadow over their lives.

It is therefore a real comfort to be able to say to such sufferers, take heart; this is not a condition of grave or hopeless meaning. It depends upon physical conditions, some within the body, others in its surroundings, which, if properly observed and respected, will prevent these attacks of languor from recurring frequently or exerting any serious influence on life.

The same reassurance may be offered to those who watch with anxiety a youth or young man whose vigor seems suddenly undermined by unaccountable weariness amid interesting work. There is no need for alarm. This is often a phase of mental development that will pass as growth proceeds, provided it is rightly understood and wisely managed.

A closer examination of the symptoms reveals their physical associations. Mental dullness is commonly accompanied by a sense of heaviness in the head and oppression of breathing, leading to yawning. At times the face feels flushed, or a limb becomes numb. Frequently there are uneasy sensations in the stomach—fullness, emptiness, or discomfort—among the familiar signs of indigestion. The muscles feel flaccid and weak. Secretions are often irregular. The hands and feet may be hot and dry, or cold and damp. The bowels are commonly sluggish, and other bodily functions diminished.

Such signs point clearly to the cause. Often it is something simple: insufficient sleep, a heavy or late supper, undue excitement, or the sudden cessation of habitual exercise. A change from an active outdoor life to sedentary indoor habits is often enough to explain such attacks. At times the use, or misuse, of tobacco is responsible. In many instances this languor is simply a form of hunger. When it appears regularly before meals, this explanation is almost certain. Nutrition is inadequate, fuel is failing, and in the brain worker this deficiency announces itself as mental languor rather than the keen hunger felt by those engaged in physical labor. One physician aptly called it the hunger of the professional man.

There are cases, however, that cannot be explained by these causes. Then it is well to look beyond the individual. Poor ventilation, stale air repeatedly breathed, air robbed of oxygen by gaslights and crowded rooms, is a fertile source of this trouble. The inefficiency of teachers and pupils in many classrooms can often be traced directly to this neglect. Mental languor arises because the blood is impoverished and cannot properly nourish the brain.

Certain atmospheric conditions also contribute powerfully to this state. Many sensitive persons are unable to do their best on foggy days with low barometric pressure, or during the oppressive stillness that precedes a summer storm. Even animals seem to share in this general depression. Whether the cause lies in excess or deficiency of ozone, no one can say with certainty; it is enough to know that something in the air is amiss.

The practical question then arises: what should be done? The answer begins with a warning, for what is commonly done is almost always wrong.

A famous writer once declared that when this disinclination to work seized him, he braced himself more firmly and forced himself to labor precisely where resistance was strongest. Such determination is admired, but it is dangerous. Violent measures of this sort often inflict serious harm.

Another common expedient is the use of stimulants – strong coffee, alcoholic drinks, or powerful tonics. This course is certainly unwise and injurious. It is equivalent to exhausting the last reserves of strength, whipping a weary horse already faint from lack of nourishment.

What ought to be done should have two aims: first, to relieve the immediate condition; second, to prevent its recurrence. For immediate relief, a complete change in the current of thought is needed. The mental appetite has grown stale through monotony; it needs variety. Lay aside the subject and take up another. Better still, cease mental labor altogether for a short time. A brisk walk in the open air, light conversation on indifferent topics, a bath followed by vigorous rubbing, will often restore energy. In cases where nourishment is lacking, a simple and nourishing refreshment will be effective. If the attacks occur at regular hours, the daily plan of work should be rearranged so that those periods are devoted to physical exercise or to a different kind of mental activity from that which previously exhausted them.

Understood in this way, mental languor ceases to be a source of needless self-reproach and anxiety. Properly managed, it need not hinder usefulness nor cast a lasting shadow over life.

For the general prevention of this condition, life must be brought more faithfully under sound sanitary rules. Ample sleep is essential; meals should be regular, simple, and moderate; excitement must be avoided; mildly laxative mineral waters may be used freely; narcotics and stimulants should be discarded; and the mental faculties employed steadily, but never driven beyond their natural limits. When these plain and well-known precautions are observed, attacks of mental languor usually diminish greatly or disappear altogether.

If, however, despite such care, the condition persists or even worsens, it is time to adopt more decisive measures. The pen and books must be laid aside, the study closed, the office locked, and health sought in the bracing air of the mountains or the free winds of lake and ocean. To persist in the struggle is both vain and dangerous.

The adversaries in such a conflict are not external; they are members of one's own household, and more than that, they belong to the inner life itself. In such a contest the risk is grave that they will prevail. Here prudence is the truest courage, and retreat becomes the surest form of victory.

What is the defeat to which this warning points? It may be expressed in the words of one of the most authoritative modern students of mental disease, Dr. Daniel Hack Tuke, who observed that one of the earliest warnings of an approaching mental breakdown is an inability to perform the same amount of intellectual work as formerly, together with a powerlessness to read even an ordinary book requiring sustained attention, increasing unfitness for the duties of life, and a growing listlessness.

End of the chapter

Chapter-9
Morbid Fear and the Struggle for Inner Courage

This chapter explains different kinds of unnecessary fears. It shows how fear can affect even brave and intelligent people. It teaches practical ways to overcome fear and build real courage.

In all ages and among all peoples, courage has been honored and cowardice despised. There is a widespread belief that in modern life personal bravery has declined. Some attribute this to long periods of peace, others to methods of warfare that, though no less destructive than those of earlier times, seldom bring men into direct personal conflict.

Whatever the explanation, it is certain that morbid and groundless fears constitute a common mental affliction for many individuals. A vague dread—often of no clearly defined object—haunts them. A sense of impending calamity makes life miserable. The fear may concern something wholly absurd, or something entirely possible; it may be as unlikely as being struck by lightning, or as inevitable as death itself. The nature of the object matters little; the terror is the same.

This condition is by no means confined to the weak or naturally timid. Not infrequently it seizes and overpowers those who have previously shown firmness of character and undaunted courage. When this occurs, it usually signals the presence, or the approach, of some physical or mental disorder. It is often associated with indigestion, sometimes with heart disease, and not rarely with nervous exhaustion brought on by overwork or lack of sleep.

At times, even strong minds develop fears that are absurd, ludicrous, or tinged with superstition. A New York merchant once crossed the street every morning to avoid stepping on a particular stone in the pavement, unable to conquer an indefinable terror attached to it. Dr. Johnson feared to enter a house unless he placed his left foot first upon the threshold—not from superstition, but from a dread he could not explain. There are many instances of people who visit a physician regarding their health and, upon reaching the office door, are afraid to ring the bell. Active business men, long accustomed to decisive action and bold ventures, become anxious and timid over trivial matters.

These groundless terrors usually assume a definite form. Though the sufferer may fully understand that the fear has no rational foundation, it nevertheless exerts such power over the imagination that it unmakes him. A medical writer once gathered and classified many of these fears occurring in persons otherwise free from mental disease. One of the most common is fear of thunderstorms. Some individuals are so overwhelmed by these natural disturbances that they close windows and doors, darken rooms, cover their heads, and attempt to shut out all sight and sound of the storm. Yet many of these people are intelligent and genuinely brave. An artillery officer, who had commanded guns with composure in battle, would surrender completely to terror during a thunderstorm and hide beneath blankets to escape its influence.

Another frequent form is fear of particular places. Some dread crossing open squares; others cannot endure crowded assemblies; still others are terrified of being alone and must constantly have companionship, though they have no need of assistance. There are those who fear performing a specific act while remaining fearless in situations of equal or greater danger. One man cannot ride a horse, yet will venture in a frail boat on rough waters. In another, the fear is reversed. In neither case does personal history justify the dread.

Few weaknesses are more common than the inability to look from a high window or over a precipice, even when a secure railing is present. The fear is not of falling, but of jumping. The sight itself tempts, and the sufferer fears yielding to the impulse.

Sometimes this fear of places or acts becomes especially distressing when it attaches to duties that must be performed:

visiting a necessary place, discussing an essential topic, or meeting an individual who must be seen.

Such cases are frequent in large cities, where men of nervous temperament are overworked, and among women whose physical strength is unequal to their social and domestic burdens.

A promising young merchant, newly married and outwardly prosperous, developed a dread of his place of business and an aversion to discussing its details. When away from home he appeared cheerful and well, but any reference to his occupation immediately made him nervous and alarmed, betraying signs of profound distress.

Others are tormented by the fear of disease or illness; some by an irrational dread of death; others profess no fear of dying, yet tremble at the thought of what dreams may come after death. This fear of the unknown future, as a great poet observed, often makes men endure present suffering rather than seek escape.

All these forms of morbid fear may exist alongside sound intellect and even apparent physical health. They signify emotional disorder, not intellectual unsoundness.

They may arise suddenly and vanish quickly, or persist as lifelong torment.

They may yield to reason and will, or be relieved through medical and hygienic measures; or they may resist all efforts.

In combating such fears, the first inquiry should be whether they rest upon a physical foundation.

Does the sufferer also complain of indigestion, exhaustion, debility, disturbed sleep, or similar ailments? If so, it is a duty to disclose these mental symptoms frankly to an intelligent and sympathetic physician and secure proper bodily treatment. Often this alone suffices to banish the haunting fears that poison day and night.

Where physical causes are absent or have been addressed, the will and reason must be summoned to the struggle.

Much can be accomplished by firm determination. Many a soldier enters battle trembling, resolved not to yield to fear, and succeeds.

One enduring maxim is worth keeping constantly in mind: the only thing truly to be feared is fear itself. When fear is conquered, its terrors vanish. A great thinker once declared that the first duty of a person is to subdue fear, for until this is done, action is crippled and thought enslaved. The measure of one's victory over fear determines the measure of one's manhood.

How is this victory to be won? What support can sustain the sufferer in this contest with an ancient and powerful enemy that still lies in wait for the weak? There is none more effective, none more constant, than that which has always sustained humanity. Let the person troubled by morbid fear accustom himself to trust calmly in the higher order governing life. Nothing is more comforting, nothing more likely to restore peace and courage, than this steadfast reliance.

End of the chapter

Chapter-10
Human Freedom
Beyond the Weight of Circumstance

This chapter explains how surroundings affect human growth. It shows the link between the body, brain, and character. It teaches that we are influenced by circumstances—but not controlled by them.

There exists a humiliating, though often excusing, view of human life that describes men and women as mere "creatures of circumstance." Every serious philosophy must acknowledge that both mind and body are profoundly influenced by surroundings, and that the conditions under which growth takes place largely shape development. Yet this truth falls far short of the claim that human beings are not only accidentally, but intentionally, nothing more than the products of external influences and physical forces acting upon a passive organism. Crude materialism presents humanity as malleable clay placed amid a rigid world, where everything except the human being exerts a shaping power, while human nature alone remains helpless and impressionable.

A doctrine that has endured through centuries usually contains an element of truth, and it cannot be denied that materialism rests upon certain undeniable facts. The question is not whether it is wholly false, but what the true limits of its truth may be. We know, from both observation and experience, that the physical nature of humanity is deeply affected by food, air, climate, and the conditions that demand the development of certain organs while allowing others to remain comparatively unused. The savage who lives chiefly by the chase acquires a strongly animal type. Those faculties required for survival become keen and vigorous, while others not immediately useful remain undeveloped. By contrast, the dweller in cities, whose food is provided and whose diet is more refined, cannot rival the savage in keenness of sight or speed of foot, but he surpasses him in powers suited to civilized life and higher mental activity. The brain, like every other organ, obeys the laws of development, and character is in large measure the moral reflection of brain activity.

The entire being of a person is also shaped by associations. Sounds, sights, and habitual impressions all contribute to personal growth. Humanity along the seacoast differs in type from that found inland, and every distinctive environment leaves its mark. Not only do habits of life influence the body, but continuous impressions from the external world guide thought into certain channels, forming habitual paths along which the mind tends to move.

It is easy to understand how widely sympathies and emotions may differ between one raised amid the rugged forces of a harsh climate and another nurtured under gentler, quieter influences.

Traits developed under these external conditions may be transmitted by inheritance, so that what began as individual peculiarities become family, national, or even racial characteristics. Over time, however, these traits are altered by new surroundings, changes of environment, and interaction with other types, until original distinctions blur and their sources become difficult to trace. Up to this point, it is clear that human beings may indeed be called creatures of circumstance.

When the student of nature traces the development of organisms throughout the animal kingdom, he observes that increasing perfection of certain organs accompanies the emergence or refinement of specific faculties.

As the organs of sense become more specialized, the senses themselves grow keener. Similarly, though less directly, development of particular regions of the brain corresponds with the manifestation of mental powers.

From these facts, the observer is justified in inferring a close connection between physical structure and mental function. What he cannot justly decide is which is cause and which is effect. One law, however, stands clear and unquestioned: development follows use.

Much confusion has arisen from misinterpretation of evolutionary teaching. Properly understood, it does not support crude materialism but rather undermines it. No organ continues to develop when it ceases to be used, and none appears where there is no demand. Muscles strengthen through labor; unused structures dwindle into insignificance. The history of life shows that animals have largely been shaped by circumstances in this way, losing what they no longer needed and developing what their conditions required. By analogy, similar principles apply to the brain. Yet in humanity we encounter a striking fact: the brain appears in a highly developed state as if prepared in advance for the service of mind. Mind does not slowly emerge as a byproduct of brain growth; rather, brain seems fashioned as an instrument for mind. Were mind merely the result of matter, development would show an unbroken chain. Instead, inquiry continually confronts the mystery of sudden emergence.

If mind were nothing more than the outcome of brain structure, every person with a large and healthy brain would be intellectual. The children of disciplined and virtuous parents would inevitably be virtuous themselves, unless external pressure intervened. Experience flatly contradicts this. We are compelled to recognize that the brain is not the essence of mind but its instrument. Mind can express itself only through the brain, and therefore even great mental power cannot exceed the capacity of the organ through which it works. The study of severe intellectual impairment illustrates this truth vividly. When access to the mind is discovered and patiently cultivated, remarkable progress can occur. The instrument was present, but the animating power had not been brought into effective use.

Science offers nothing that should weaken confidence in the existence of mind or soul—however named—standing behind the physical frame. The faculties of body and brain serve as channels through which this inner power communicates with the world. A better instrument allows wider expression, but the quality of performance cannot fully measure the power behind it. Apparent defects may arise from the instrument itself or from lack of active energy.

Human beings are creatures of circumstance only within limits. Circumstances exert strong influence, but they neither explain nor excuse defects of character, nor do they lessen personal responsibility. Those who seek shelter from self-reproach by invoking circumstance search for refuge where none exists. It is a fundamental duty to resist the tyranny of surroundings. When conditions are favorable, they confer no merit; when they are adverse, the noble task is to rise above them. True worth lies in mastering circumstances rather than submitting to them.

The degrading notion that human nature is wholly plastic should be rejected by every instinct of self-respect. Inner consciousness assures us that we can struggle, resist, and endure, even when victory is uncertain. Much harm has been done to weak minds by the timid doctrine that humans are merely the products of circumstance. It is time to discard that enfeebling maxim and replace it with one of greater dignity and truth. Human beings are not the slaves of circumstance; they are its masters. What they have not created, they can subdue and employ in the service of higher and more honorable ends.

End of the chapter

Part–2

The Inner Architecture of a Clear and Steady Mind

This part turns from mental disturbance to mental order. Having examined the common troubles that cloud thought and weaken vitality, the discussion now moves toward the deeper principles that sustain clarity, balance, and enduring intellectual strength.

Here the reader is guided through the quiet laws that govern mental well-being—laws that operate continuously, whether understood or ignored. The influence of bodily heat on sensibility, the subtle power of habit over action, the moral significance of how we measure time, and the deeply personal nature of pleasure are explored as forces shaping daily consciousness. These are not abstract ideas, but practical realities that determine whether the mind remains lucid or becomes fatigued and confused.

This section also addresses those inner distortions that most often undermine clarity: exaggerated self-importance, misunderstood consistency, and the loss of simplicity in character. It shows how false notions of strength—rigidity, pride, restless ambition—gradually impair judgment, while true mental power arises from simplicity of aim, integrity of purpose, and steadiness of will.

Part 2 brings these elements together to reveal the foundations of a clear head. Mental clarity is shown not as a gift or accident, but as the natural outcome of orderly habits, truthful self-assessment, disciplined pleasure, and single-minded conduct. When these principles are understood and lived, the mind regains command of itself, work becomes lighter, thought more exact, and life more intelligible and humane.

This section completes the journey from strain to steadiness, offering not formulas or tricks, but a framework for living with sustained intellectual health and inner composure.

Chapter-1
The Laws of Heat and Their Influence on Human Sensibility

This chapter explains how the body produces and controls heat. It shows the difference between feeling warm and actual temperature. It teaches practical rules for health, clothing, and climate care.

Expressions such as a "cool head" or being "hot-headed" are commonly applied to temperament rather than to actual bodily temperature; yet, for a clear understanding of the subject before us, it is necessary to explain, at least briefly, the principles of animal heat and the laws that govern temperature, both real and perceived.

Heat itself and the sensation of heat are by no means identical. When, on a cold day or after washing in cold water, a person rubs his hands until they glow, there is in reality only a slight rise in temperature produced by friction. The warmth felt is chiefly the result of nervous excitement mechanically stimulated by the rubbing. Immediately afterward, the blood flows more freely into the excited parts, as shown by the redness; but the initial impression of warmth is mainly one of sensation. Feeling and fact, therefore, are not constantly related. A person may feel hot when both the surrounding air and the actual temperature of the body are low, or may feel cold when the body is in truth overheated. Such perverted sensations may form part of disease, or they may arise from individual peculiarities that render certain perceptions unusually acute. Conversely, there are conditions in which the sense of heat is dulled, and even considerable elevations of temperature pass unnoticed. It is evident, therefore, how unreliable mere sensation is as a guide to the true thermal state of the body or its surroundings.

The animal body generates its own heat and, to a large extent, is independent of external conditions.

If properly protected from excessive cooling or heating influences, it will maintain a nearly uniform and healthful temperature. Food is the source of this heat. In the subtle processes of life it acts as fuel, undergoing oxidation or, in plain terms, combustion. When food is insufficient or unsuitable, or when digestion and assimilation are impaired, the body fails to generate adequate heat from within, and the individual experiences cold. Much has been written about foods especially suited to heat production. While it is true that substances rich in fat tend to generate warmth, practical experience shows that whatever nourishes the body also warms it.

The production of heat is not confined to any single organ. Neither lungs nor liver serves as a central furnace. Heat is generated throughout the body. The blood is not merely a carrier of warmth; it is itself a producer of heat. It holds in solution the prepared elements of food absorbed from the digestive organs and distributes them to the tissues, where they are used to replace material consumed in vital activity. Each tissue selects, through the delicate network of capillary vessels, what it requires. In this chemico-vital process, new combinations occur and heat is set free.

When the amount of material appropriated exceeds the needs of the system, or when nutrition is carried on too rapidly—perhaps because tissues have been previously exhausted or starved—excessive heat may result. If this excess is general, fever arises; if local, inflammation appears. Disturbance of nutrition, whether caused by chill, injury, or poison, establishes disease, and increased temperature is one of its immediate effects. Conversely, when nutrition is defective or fails altogether, the opposite abnormal state occurs: deficiency of heat. The vital processes are imperfectly carried on, and the bodily temperature falls, as in starvation.

Wherever humans live—under tropical suns or arctic cold—the internal temperature necessary for health remains essentially the same, about 98.4 to 98.6 degrees Fahrenheit. Even slight deviation from this standard indicates or constitutes disease.

External heat plays only a secondary role; it cannot compensate for deficiencies in the heat generated within the body. Except temporarily, such as in warming a chilled surface and preventing further loss, external heat is useless for vital purposes.

When a chilled person enters a warm room or sits before a fire, benefit is derived only until the skin reaches its normal temperature. Beyond that point the body strives to rid itself of excess heat, chiefly by perspiration. Any heat added above the normal standard is wasteful and potentially harmful, except insofar as it promotes sweating, which may help eliminate burdensome or morbid materials. This principle explains the usefulness of Turkish baths and other forms of induced perspiration, which stimulate the skin and open additional channels of elimination.

It follows that in fever the surrounding air should be cool, while in depressing illnesses marked by deficient heat production the environment should be warm.

These conclusions agree precisely with long clinical experience and observation.

Clothing itself contains no heat. Warmth comes from the body, from the surrounding air, or from substances in contact with the skin. Garments can absorb and retain heat according to their capacity, and this property determines their value as clothing. The second essential quality is the ability of a fabric to hold the heat it has absorbed. Some materials warm quickly and retain heat longer than others under identical conditions.

The guiding principle of dress is therefore to protect the body from external influences that draw heat away when the surrounding temperature is lower than that of the body, and to shield it from excessive heat when external conditions exceed the body's own temperature.

The absorption of heat by the body is governed by the degree to which the body is colder than its surroundings. As already noted, the organism requires no more external heat than is sufficient to raise it to about 98.4 or 98.6 degrees Fahrenheit, and even this assistance may often be dispensed with when there is no undue loss of heat from within.

Practically speaking, therefore, we have little need to absorb heat from external sources. In a temperate yet variable climate, our chief concern should be to conserve the heat we generate during winter, and to defend ourselves, by moderate and intelligent means, from excessive heat in summer, rather than to devise elaborate safeguards against either extreme. Nature herself assigns greater importance to internal heat than to variations of external temperature.

Thus, she has given the inhabitants of tropical regions dark skins, which radiate heat more freely than white, despite the fact that darker colors absorb heat more rapidly. Conversely, she has given the dwellers of polar regions pale skins, and clothed the polar bear in white fur, because white parts less readily with the heat it contains or covers.

Radiation of heat occurs whenever the surrounding environment is cooler than the body. In a living organism, the aim must therefore be to prevent heat from escaping too rapidly. This consideration guides the choice of materials and colors for clothing—those which retain warmth in winter, and those which resist excessive heat in summer.

Reflection, in practice, is closely allied to radiation, though with this distinction: a reflecting surface may repel heat without itself becoming appreciably warm, whereas a radiating body must first be charged with heat before it can give it off. Evaporation, however, is the chief cooling process of the body. Perspiration reduces temperature precisely because, as the fluid passes into vapor, it carries heat away from the skin. Nature employs this same principle when she bathes the surface of the body with sweat, just as we artificially cool an object by sprinkling it with water.

In this way sweating lowers bodily temperature in fever, and, when the cause of mischief has exhausted itself or the poison has run its course, brings relief.

Earlier physicians laid greater stress than we do today on what they termed "critical sweatings," yet it remains true that when febrile diseases terminate naturally, copious perspiration commonly appears at the crisis, and the evaporation that follows aids materially in reducing heat.

Heat may also be reduced by other discharges, but internal discharges generally indicate that some organ has accumulated materials the system cannot assimilate.

For milder febrile disturbances, Nature prefers surface evaporation, and it is usually sufficient.

Local temperature—the heat of particular regions of the body—is determined chiefly by the circulation of the blood and the activity of nutrition.

Where the blood flows freely, heat is maintained; where its flow is impeded, temperature falls. Anyone may verify this by wearing tight gloves on a cold day. The pressure restricts circulation, and the hands grow cold.

There is no warmth in the gloves themselves; they merely prevent the escape of heat generated within.

Similarly, if a cloth soaked in cold water is laid on the skin and covered with an impervious or non-conducting material, the heat of the body will raise the water to the point at which it becomes vapor as soon as the covering is removed. When extremities are enclosed in dense coverings, their warmth depends entirely on the heat produced within them; if circulation is hindered, nothing is gained and much is lost by external protection.

This principle has great practical importance. The feet cannot be kept warm unless blood circulates freely through them, and this will not occur if shoes, boots, or stockings are tight. Stockings are often the worst offenders.

Closely fitting garments that exert pressure at the instep, ankle, or knee inevitably obstruct circulation and diminish natural warmth. Although it is sometimes argued that such pressure supports the veins and aids the return of blood to the heart, experience proves otherwise. Tight stockings almost invariably mean cold feet, and much habitual chilliness arises from constriction caused by garters or ill-fitting hosiery.

There is a popular belief that cold feet imply a hot head, and that warming the extremities draws blood away from the brain and cools it. Those familiar with fever and with the habits of peoples who leave their extremities uncovered know that this theory is only partially true.

Heat depends on nutrition and activity. Active tissues demand nourishment and generate warmth. When feet are left bare, the muscles of the foot and leg work freely; the arch flexes, the toes engage in movement, circulation is stimulated, nutrition is promoted, and heat is maintained. When the foot is immobilized and compressed, no amount of external warmth will compensate for the lack of internal activity. Throughout the body, work is both the cause and the counterpart of heat.

The same principle applies to the head. External cooling alone cannot permanently reduce heat if the brain itself is excessively or disorderedly active. The brain is the most delicate and continuously working organ of the body. Its tissue changes rapidly in proportion to its activity, and it demands constant and prompt nutrition. Even in sleep it is rarely wholly at rest, as dreams attest. When the head feels hot, there is almost always a local cause, and the remedy must address that cause directly. Temporary relief may be gained by warming the extremities, but unless special conditions exist, the true source of head-heat is undue exertion or disturbed nutrition in the brain. The strain may even be confined to a particular sensory apparatus, as when prolonged reading or strong light overheats the organs of sight. In such cases, relief lies in reducing or altering the kind of mental or sensory activity that has been excessive.

From these considerations we may draw several conclusions. First, bodily heat depends far more on internal conditions and functions than on external temperature.

The human organism possesses a remarkable power of self-regulation, and our chief aim should be to support rather than thwart this natural capacity. Second, external temperature should be regarded more as a challenge than as a helper. If we rely on warmth from without to sustain warmth within, we become dependent and vulnerable to every change of climate.

A body that reacts poorly to cold is not in full health; it lacks sufficient heat-producing power, unless some temporary cause of waste can be clearly shown.

Third, the maintenance of a healthy temperature rests chiefly on a free and well-distributed circulation of blood rich in nourishing materials.

A healthy heart is the first condition of such circulation, unimpeded by mental or physical irritants. Sudden fear or grief can arrest the flow of blood and produce chill; prolonged anxiety may retard it permanently.

The mind exerts a direct influence on the heart and blood-vessels, narrowing or widening the small arteries, as seen in blushing or pallor. Instead of burdening the body with excessive clothing, those who are habitually cold should seek the underlying physical cause. The blood must circulate freely, be well nourished, and free from toxic burdens. Excess of any single element may impair the whole. It is a common error among the chronically unwell to dose themselves with supposed "heating" or "cooling" substances. The body does not need such artificial management. Proper nourishment, orderly function, and intelligent self-care will secure health far more surely than any contrivance of stimulants or refrigerants.

End of the chapter

Chapter-2
Habit and the Hidden Governance of Action

This chapter explains how habits are formed. It shows how actions can be done without conscious thought. It teaches how habit can both help and mislead the mind.

It is surprising, on careful examination, to discover how large a share of the actions we perform—actions that seem to be directed and controlled by the will—are in reality carried out unconsciously. Walking, running, leaping, lifting, and carrying burdens—indeed, most movements involving t.

he muscular system—are executed without conscious attention to their details. We perceive the end alone; the will is occupied with the result and ignores the steps by which it is achieved. We set out to walk along a certain road toward a definite destination; the legs and feet are set in motion, and we continue onward while the mind is absorbed in thought, giving no heed to the management of the limbs unless some unusual sensation calls attention to them. We carry a book or a parcel and hold it securely, though we may entirely forget that we are doing so. In short, there exists within us a power of setting parts of the organism to work and leaving their execution to a subordinate agency that acts without our conscious supervision.

Consider a familiar example. Once or twice each day most of us lift a water jug from a washstand. We intend to pour water and expect to find the jug filled. The muscular movements required to grasp the handle and raise the vessel are performed automatically, and just the amount of force needed to lift the usual weight is applied. If, however, the jug has been left empty, it rises abruptly with a sudden bound. Or again, when walking upstairs, habit leads us to expect another step at the top; the leg is raised, and the foot comes down sharply when the anticipated stair is not there. In descending, the reverse may occur: the foot is checked by the level floor when another step was expected. These commonplace mishaps are familiar to all, yet they are deeply significant, for they exemplify a wide class of actions that are performed unconsciously. The very nature of these mistakes reveals the unconscious character of the process.

When an action is performed for the first time, the will must direct every step. Each movement is intentional, as when a child learns to walk, or a pianist learns to strike the correct keys with the appropriate fingers in proper rhythm. Once the combination of acts is mastered, the will no longer supervises the performance. Attention is withdrawn, and indeed must be diverted, for the action is now entrusted to a subordinate faculty. Anyone who doubts this may try to perform consciously what habit ordinarily accomplishes without thought—such as descending a staircase while deliberately attending to the placing of each foot, or striking a series of musical chords while carefully directing every finger.

The result is embarrassment, awkwardness, and sometimes complete failure. This occurs because the will has learned to delegate the control of habitual movements to an inferior guiding faculty which, though incapable of originating action, is perfectly able to repeat familiar combinations. Having thus delegated its authority, the will ceases to concern itself with these details, and they pass out of conscious awareness.

In certain pathological conditions this delegation fails. The muscles then refuse to act unless each movement is directly willed. Physiologists record the case of a nurse who could not hold a child in her arms unless she kept her attention constantly fixed upon it; the moment her thoughts wandered, her arms relaxed and the child fell. This striking instance illustrates the principle clearly. Much of what we do is done unconsciously; and in proportion as actions become habitual, they are more likely to pass beyond the reach of consciousness.

What, then, is habit? It is often said, by those who excuse human weakness, that habit is second nature. It would be more accurate to say that habit is memory reinforced by a form of unconscious reasoning—a simple inference from past experience to present action. The phrase "unconscious reasoning" is used deliberately. There is strong evidence that certain forms of reasoning can proceed without the intervention of judgment or the awareness of the higher intellect. While the mind is engaged with one subject, subordinate faculties may be actively at work on another, even completing processes which, when reviewed later, appear complex. This explains how the sleepwalker adapts his actions to surrounding circumstances while the brain is asleep and consciousness suspended. Such reasoning closely resembles instinct in animals, which often seems to rival deliberate judgment.

At the heart of habit lies an unconscious expectation that events will conform to previous experience. This expectation governs conduct and determines the amount and kind of effort applied. In lifting the water jug, the force exerted is exactly that which experience has taught us is sufficient for the expected weight. There is no conscious calculation; the subordinate faculty reasons from past to present. That something more than memory is involved is shown by the fact that while an empty jug is lifted too forcibly, a smaller jug is never raised with the excessive force suitable for a larger one. The eye supplies information, and the appropriate amount of effort is unconsciously adjusted. In both cases the act is performed without conscious thought. Similarly, a man walking absorbed in thought may stumble over a shadow. Before he is aware of it, the shadow has deceived the instinctive faculty and prompted unnecessary movements, which result in the stumble.

Habit in the muscular system consists in the repetition of acts previously performed. These range from meaningless grimaces to highly ordered and even complex actions carried out with precision while the mind is elsewhere engaged. A skilled worker may continue his task, making delicate adjustments, while his thoughts wander far away; only afterward does he notice with surprise what he has accomplished. A turner at the lathe may fashion a perfectly formed ball when he intended to make a socket. His hands worked by habit while his mind was occupied elsewhere.

Mental habit follows the same laws and is subject to similar errors. An accountant, preoccupied with other thoughts, may add instead of subtracting or multiply instead of dividing. The work is accurately done—but it is the wrong operation. His mind has wandered from the purpose of the task, leaving a subordinate faculty to carry out a familiar process of reasoning, incapable of originating the correct motive idea required by the end in view.

Countless misunderstandings would be avoided if these errors of unconscious reasoning were better understood. Unfortunately, it is exceedingly difficult to make the mind aware of its own unconscious operations.

The intellect resists the admission that it ever relaxes its vigilance and fails to recognize that many of its functions are performed by proxy. Most people are astonished, even offended, when told that they do not spell consciously. Yet the fact is evident: to be sure of the spelling of many words, we must write them. Writing is an automatic act, like playing a chord on an instrument, and only by performing it under the guidance of habit—and then inspecting the result—do we achieve certainty that deliberate judgment alone cannot provide.

Further confirmation of this view may be obtained by a simple experiment. Try to spell a word in writing by means of an unfamiliar instrument—for example, a typewriter or a telegraph key. Persons who have long been regarded as accurate spellers and sound etymologists often discover, when they attempt to strike the letters rapidly in such a manner, that they stumble over the simplest combinations. This does not occur in every case, but it is sufficiently common to be both striking and instructive. Spelling, like many other operations, has become an unconscious act; and when the will is suddenly required to resume a task it has long entrusted to a subordinate faculty, it proves unequal to the duty without renewed training.

What is true of the arrangement of letters into words is equally true of the arrangement of words into sentences. Those who have acquired the habit of speaking extemporaneously rarely write with the same ease, and the converse is no less frequent. Authors and orators alike tend to repeat themselves, and men who have written or spoken for many years accumulate a store of phrases which instinct employs with such speed and certainty that it often takes the place of genuine thought. Given a subject, sentences are strung together with little apparent effort, and the higher intellectual faculties are scarcely called into play. Writing, under such conditions, can proceed almost as if the mind were asleep.

There are well-authenticated instances in which writers have composed articles that were coherent and even well expressed while in a state bordering on mental unconsciousness, and certainly with the smallest possible expenditure of deliberate thought. This duality of mental power varies greatly among individuals. Some can do little or nothing without a direct and conscious exertion of the will; others can perform almost any familiar task without conscious effort at all. To be "a practiced hand" is simply to have transferred the work to the instinctive or subordinate intelligence below the level of the will; and it is both scientifically possible and practically demonstrable that what is done in this way may, under particular conditions, be done unconsciously.

This consideration leads directly to the conclusion toward which the argument has been tending. Unconscious energy, guided by habit and instinct, is capable of producing results that appear astonishing, and it furnishes a sufficient explanation of many phenomena commonly described as spiritualistic or somnambulistic "manifestations." It is neither necessary nor scientific to assume that those concerned in many apparent impostures—using the word to describe the nature of the act rather than the intention—are guilty of deliberate deception. Take, for example, the so-called "medium." It is by no means certain that automatic writing or trance-speaking is a conscious fraud. Habits are easily formed, and among the easiest is the habit of speaking or writing without thinking.

The process by which such feats are accomplished is precisely that already described—the delegation of control to a lower faculty, which is allowed to act independently of conscious supervision, and ultimately without consciousness at all. Once such a habit is established, it becomes entirely possible for the individual himself, or for another person, to distract or suspend his attention, even to the point of inducing sleep, while the subordinate intelligence remains active. In this state it can carry on simple reasoning, show a certain ingenuity, and even make partial use of the senses. This is the condition of the somnambulist, and in some cases it can be produced at will, either by the subject himself or through the influence of another. What are known as mesmeric passes, or any other means of diverting the mind and signaling the intention, may be employed; once consciousness is withdrawn, the lower faculty is left free to act.

The range of this instinctive intelligence is limited to memory and the simpler forms of inference; but practice can undoubtedly give it a deceptive appearance of enlarged capacity. The manner in which mediums and somnambulists are trained may be understood by observing what occurs in those who talk in their sleep. It is often possible to converse with such persons by carefully framed questions, without awakening them. The same principle operates, though in reverse order, when a medium is put to sleep while his subordinate reasoning faculty is engaged in the business of a séance.

A weak or morbid mental condition favors the production of these states, and each repetition renders the diversion of consciousness more easy. The essential point is that the performer is genuinely unconscious, and may sincerely believe himself to be under supernatural influence. The same explanation applies to table-turning. The participants are unaware of the physical force they exert; once movement begins, all present may unconsciously contribute to it. Unconscious mental activity and involuntary muscular action are, in truth, exceedingly common, and they sufficiently explain effects that otherwise seem mysterious and are hastily attributed to agencies of whose existence we have no evidence.

The practical and moral lesson to be drawn from these facts is a warning. It is neither wise nor safe, in the interest of mental health, to push the habit of unconscious action beyond reasonable limits. People are naturally proud of becoming experts, and they readily take credit for automatic dexterity. The pianist who executes the most intricate passages without error may glory in his skill, though he possess little genuine musical feeling. The author who can produce book after book with astonishing rapidity is applauded for his industry, although much of his work may be mechanical.

The world judges by results and seldom inquires into methods. Whether a piece of work is produced by deliberate thought or by instinctive repetition, whether it represents genuine intellectual labor or unconscious routine, is of little concern to those who merely appraise the finished product. Yet those who value mental vigor and clarity will do well to rely less on automatic processes and to give intentional thought a larger share in their work.

A considerable portion of human energy must necessarily be entrusted to the lower intelligence; but the more steadily the mind is kept upon the task in hand, the more consistently one thing is done at a time and done thoroughly, the less the individual will be dominated by habit. Habit will then remain under the control of the will, and the danger will be diminished of that separation between higher reason and instinctive action which so often ends in mental disorder, leaving the sufferer divided against himself—a confused brain-worker, or, in extreme cases, a monomaniac.

End of the chapter

Chapter-3
The Human Sense of Time and Its Moral Meaning

This chapter explains why time feels fast or slow. It shows how our thoughts change our sense of time. It teaches how to live so that time feels full and meaningful.

Nature herself sets the primary measures of time—day and night, month and season—and we merely refine her method by dividing the day into hours and minutes, and the year into its familiar portions.

Our system of timekeeping is, in this sense, artificial, though more exact than Nature's own broad divisions as far as conscious experience is concerned.

Yet it is under her guidance, and at her prompting, that we mark the passage of time at all; without such landmarks it would glide by unnoticed in its uniform flow.

Scientific inquiry would be impossible without some method of measuring time; the operations of thought would become vague and unbounded; and life itself would sink to little more than bare existence, stripped of hope for the future, interest in the present, and clear remembrance of the past. If the reckoning of time were lost, and with it the power of making fresh records, domestic life would be disordered, exploration impracticable, and chaos would take the place of order. For humanity, the world would relapse into a state "without form and void."

The faculty of measuring time is instinctive, though perfected and applied through knowledge. It exists even among the most primitive races; tribes that cannot count beyond a few numbers still possess the power of observing lapse and change, and of estimating duration in some practical way. It is not, however, the natural history or the scientific mechanics of timekeeping that concern us here, but rather a deeper mental and moral aspect of the subject.

Most people are familiar with the curious differences in the apparent rate at which time passes. How unlike are its movements under varying conditions, amid different circumstances, or to opposite temperaments placed in the same situation. Even the same mind, in different moods, experiences time as either dragging heavily or flying swiftly. These variations are so universally recognized that they need no illustration. We must remember, however, that the "progress of time" is a figure of speech. Time itself does not hasten or delay; it is our estimate of its passage that varies. The very discrepancies in our judgments make it necessary to adopt a common measure by which experience can be compared. Yet the causes of these discrepancies are instructive.

At the root of the matter lies a simple truth. Time resembles a chain: if we count it link by link, it appears long; if we pass lightly along it to the end, it seems short. When every link is regarded as an obstacle or a stage to be endured before reaching a desired goal, the passage feels slow and burdensome. When each link is seen as a step bringing us nearer the end, the journey appears rapid. Much depends on the nature of that end. If it is eagerly desired, the counting of stages becomes wearisome; if it is dreaded, the links seem to slip through the fingers with alarming speed.

This general rule explains many experiences that might otherwise appear contradictory. No one welcomes pain, yet the time immediately preceding a surgical operation often seems intolerably slow.

The mind is not fixed on the pain itself, but on the moment beyond it, when relief will come and the ordeal will be past. The same principle explains the difference in the way death is approached by those who have hope of a future and those who have none. When a bright expectation lies beyond, attention is directed forward, and death becomes the final stage of a journey one longs to complete. When hope is absent, or death appears as a calamity or punishment, it becomes the object of dread, and the time leading to it seems to rush by too quickly.

The mental process at work may be described as one of concentration. When attention is fixed on details, and each small incident claims notice, time appears to move slowly. When the end alone occupies the mind, intermediate events are felt as hindrances, and the interval seems endlessly prolonged. The same principle explains the contrast between past and future. Looking backward, we lose sight of the daily procession of events, and the past seems short. Looking forward, the future is crowded with plans and purposes that draw the mind along the path and give a sense of distance. If a single longed-for object fixes attention—such as the freedom imagined by youth in the years ahead—the road to it is scarcely seen, and the goal appears near. In every case the experience is subjective, depending entirely on the mental attitude.

Though the present moment seems elusive, there are states in which time drags like a heavy chain over a weary spirit, and others in which the mind moves so joyously that hours pass unnoticed.

These sensations are determined by the same conditions. They depend on how the mind regards its surroundings, its prospects, and its memories—on whether it feels hurried onward or held back. In this sense there is a real mental awareness of the passing instant, and therefore a true present.

What practical meaning do these reflections have for life as it is lived? To make time seem full and long in retrospect, it must be filled with incidents that engage attention and leave clear traces in memory. Few lives are entirely without experience, but those that are least varied, and especially those that lack purpose or inspiration, appear longest when viewed from the outset and shortest when looked back upon. The future stretches ahead as an immeasurable vista because it is unmarked; the past lies behind like a faint track across a desert, soon lost to sight. Mark that path with milestones, and it becomes pleasant and distinct to retrace in thought. The more numerous the records, the longer and clearer the journey appears.

Painful memories also lengthen the retrospect, but they do so by producing weariness rather than a sense of maturity. Happy and useful experiences, on the other hand, give the feeling of having lived fully, of possessing strength gained through experience rather than exhaustion from suffering. In either case, it is the busy life that seems longest—whether the activity be noble or ignoble, beneficial or harmful. Time, as it is felt and remembered, is shaped less by its duration than by the manner in which it is lived.

The lesson to be drawn from these considerations is so clear that it scarcely requires argument. Those who wish to carry into later life a sense of contented maturity—when the consciousness of declining strength inevitably appears—must live with purpose and dignity while life is still young and vigorous. Nothing prepares the mind for rest so surely as the knowledge that one has labored toward a worthy end. Those who can look back upon a full record of work honestly accomplished enjoy the feeling of having lived long and well, and they are best fitted to lay down the responsibilities of life with the satisfaction of duty fulfilled and with the least regret or disappointment in surrendering them.

The same principle applies equally to the present and the future. If we desire time to pass lightly, without that painful sense of being burdened or weary—without being driven to the unhappy expedients of trying to "pass time" or "kill time," which embitter the lives of so many—there is but one remedy: the mind must be earnestly fixed upon some object worthy of effort. Mere occupation is not enough. As we have already seen, industry alone may even make time seem heavier, by turning the daily round of duty into a series of oppressive obstacles. This explains why many ease-loving people find no relief from the weight of life in work. Their labor has no purpose. It absorbs the attention without inspiring hope, and instead of carrying time forward, it clogs and exhausts the spirit.

Work without purpose inevitably has this effect. It forces the mind to count the hours until the task is done, while the soul wears itself away and the slow foot of time appears not to move at all. But when work brings energy and hope, when it lightens darkness and brightens the day, it possesses a true end. The mind no longer regards it as unrewarded toil, but as a means to something beyond itself, on which the eye of expectation is steadily fixed. Life, if it is to be happy, must have an object and a future. Nothing else can sweeten it or make it move with ease and vigor.

It is well that custom has set up milestones along the road of life, marking the passage of years and offering each traveler a standard by which to judge personal progress. With every such reminder that another period has passed, a crowd of searching questions presses upon the mind. Has the year just ended gone more swiftly or more slowly than those before it? Because its events are fresh in memory, while earlier details may have faded, judgment is easily misled into thinking the recent past busier or better spent than it truly was. Allowance must be made for this defect in the register kept by conscience.

It is usually an unfavorable sign when the recent past seems short and the near future long. Such an estimate suggests weakness of spirit, or the absence of cherished memories—no solid body of work on which the mind can rest with pleasure, no legitimate pride born of honorable effort. The way in which each person measures time is deeply significant, and, if fairly interpreted, throws a strong light on character. People reckon time very differently. The young and the old, the virtuous and the careless, look upon past and future from opposite standpoints and under very different aspects.

It is a happy and hopeful state when the years gone by appear like ripe sheaves safely garnered, while the future seems all too short for the work yet to be done, the happiness yet to be enjoyed, and the worthy prize that still shines in the distance to be won by faithful service.

The priceless virtue of patience reveals itself in a wise and self-possessed way of measuring time. Much of the pain and sorrow of impatience arises from an inability to perform this natural, half-unconscious function in respectful harmony with the laws that govern the orderly succession of causes and effects. The cultivation of this noble quality—the power to wait—is one of the chief aims of education and of self-discipline.

True patience is not the harsh repression of desire, but the ability to give due attention to means and processes without losing sight of the end. The goal is kept steadily before the mind, while the intellect occupies itself with the steps by which it is to be reached.

The wise person does not lie idle in helpless expectancy. He works while he waits, and whatever he undertakes contributes, directly or indirectly, to the purpose that animates him. He is not blind to the passage of time nor insensible to its slowness, but he shortens the apparent delay by filling the interval with useful actions that advance his aim, engage the mind, and do not exhaust it. Patience is an active, not a passive, quality. It renews energy instead of wasting it. The mistaken notion that waiting means sitting still has been the cause of countless failures. Those who are truly patient are always at work, turning strength into progress, bringing their hopes nearer fulfillment, and making the road seem shorter by enriching it with worthy achievements that absorb thought and protect the mind from disappointment and weariness.

No one can escape the daily task of measuring time. Those who pretend to ignore it are either oppressed by its seeming slowness or startled by the sudden discovery of how swiftly it has flown. The only way to live calmly and contentedly—free from boredom on the one hand and unpleasant surprises on the other—is to make the reckoning of time a matter of thoughtful attention. A person who deliberately neglects the state of his affairs deserves the misfortune that overtakes him.

He purchases the ease of ignorance at the cost of constant risk and ultimate failure. Those who attempt to disregard the flight of time make an even worse bargain.

They pay for their indifference with a present sense of heaviness and weariness that nothing can relieve except purpose and steady effort. Their hearts are not at peace in solitude, and their minds are seldom clear.

End of the chapter

Chapter-4
The Personal Nature of Pleasure

This chapter explains why people enjoy different things. It shows how temperament and thought affec happiness. It teaches that the ability to enjoy life can be shaped and developed.

The saying that no one can do good work unless he takes pleasure in what he is doing is especially true of every form of intellectual labor, and indeed of all activities in which the mind plays the leading part.

Yet tastes differ widely, not only in the objects from which individuals derive happiness, but also in the conditions under which enjoyment is possible. Some people draw pleasure from the simplest sources and can transform even adverse circumstances into occasions of contentment. Others must, as it were, be lifted out of their habitual surroundings and inspired by a new influence before they can be said to enjoy life or experience genuine happiness.

The same source of pleasure may affect different individuals in wholly different ways, even when all are equally attracted to it. One may be stirred to enthusiastic delight by its contemplation; another may be led into a train of reflections that awaken kindly and generous feelings, yet remain inward and unshared; a third may appear scarcely moved at all, while nevertheless experiencing a quiet and deeply personal enjoyment. These differences, and the countless forms in which they appear, illustrate the extraordinary variety of the sense of pleasure or happiness—an experience as diverse in kind as it is in degree.

Pleasure is a state of mind. It depends less on the object or circumstance that occasions it than on the constitution and temperament of the person who feels it. What once stirred us profoundly at a particular stage of life, or in a certain mood, may later leave us indifferent, or even provoke distaste or melancholy, under altered conditions of time, place, or feeling. Not only do different people respond differently; the same individual may experience entirely different emotions when confronted with the same scene, story, entertainment, or object of taste at different periods of life.

The capacity for enjoyment is personal, much like the power of a musical instrument to produce sound.

A skilled performer will draw finer tones from a well-constructed instrument than from one that is defective; yet, just as some musicians can coax melody from the most unpromising materials, so even those least favored by temperament may, under certain conditions, be stirred to something like pleasure. Still, the capacity itself—the sensitivity to agreeable impressions and the power to enjoy them—is part of human nature. Like every other faculty, it varies in sharpness according to the development it has received through training, circumstance, or deliberate cultivation.

It is fashionable to speak of the "means of happiness" as though they possessed an inherent power to delight all alike. When an expected response is not forthcoming, the person who fails to be amused is often pitied or reproached for supposed dullness or insensibility. In reality, his nature may be keenly responsive to pleasure, while the particular stimulus offered simply happens to be uncongenial.

The influence of temperament and habits of thought on the capacity for enjoyment is often underestimated. A mind trained to view life with severe realism and a strong sense of responsibility may lose the ability to take pleasure in works of fiction or imaginative entertainment, while remaining keenly responsive to wit and humor that do not distort social realities. Without this explanation, it may seem strange that thoughtful and capable individuals, burdened daily with grave and even gloomy views of life, can be amused by trivial pleasantries, while entertainments that delight others of lesser intellectual power leave them untouched.

The habit of stripping away illusion, of penetrating the glamour cast by social conventions, and of analyzing conduct and motive, gradually weakens the enjoyment that others derive from artificial portrayals of character and fictitious scenes. The lawyer is dissatisfied with a drama that violates sound principles of conduct and legal procedure; the anatomist is offended by a painting or statue that disregards proportion and form; the physician finds no pleasure in colors and shapes that to him signify disease. In the same way, as observation deepens with experience, many lose patience with the inaccuracies of unreal drama, and the stage loses its charm. As years pass, scenes once associated with pleasure become linked with painful memories, and sorrow rather than joy is awakened by their recall.

Thus the habit of reflection often stands in the way of commonplace pleasures. The habit of looking forward into the future may be even more destructive. Few things, for example, are less conducive to the simple enjoyment expected from a theatrical performance than the intrusion of the thought that the actors, after their brief hour upon the stage of life, must one day lay aside their roles forever. Such reflections shatter illusion, and, arising unbidden in the midst of light entertainment, extinguish its charm. For some minds, what appears to others as an occasional and passing thought becomes a constant keynote, rendering them incapable of enjoying certain amusements, though their susceptibility to pleasure from other sources remains unimpaired.

The opposite temperament illustrates the power of habit in sharpening enjoyment derived from imagination and fiction. It is often remarked that actors themselves are especially fond of the theatre, in marked contrast to members of other professions, who usually seek diversion far from the scenes of their daily labor. The explanation likely lies in the habit of assuming characters and living, as it were, in a world of imagined sentiment. This practice develops a special sensitivity to imaginative pleasure, until the unreal almost supplants the real.

In everyday life, the contrast is often striking: the comedian may be a melancholy figure, while the tragedian delights in humorous views of existence, as temperament or mood dictates.

Habit is as influential in shaping preferences for particular forms of enjoyment as it is in determining their intensity. Children and young people who grow up surrounded by associations that link pleasure with certain scenes and activities naturally seek enjoyment in those same objects and pursuits. The tastes of country life differ from those of the city or the sea, and people trained exclusively in one environment often fail to understand the enthusiasm of those formed by another. Yet the faculty of enjoyment is the same in all, and may be equally keen, though developed in such a specialized direction as to be insensitive to impressions outside its accustomed range.

Pleasure is infinite in its variety, and there is scarcely any form of excitement that has not at times been enlisted in its service. This simple fact strikes at the root of the notion of pure self-mortification or absolute self-denial. Human nature is so fundamentally governed by self-interest that it is unreasonable to suppose anyone ever truly denies his strongest inclination. Whatever impulse is gratified in any act of life must, at least for the moment, be the dominant one; otherwise it would not prevail over competing desires.

The only sense in which a person can truthfully be said to deny himself—that is, to deprive himself of the pleasure he most desires—is when, by some prior pledge or deliberate act of self-restraint, he has placed it beyond his power to gratify a particular wish or inclination. Even then, it was his pleasure to make that sacrifice at the moment it was undertaken. The act itself yielded a form of enjoyment, though it carried with it the prospect of future pain. The common rhetoric of self-sacrifice, therefore, will not bear close examination. The pleasure of renunciation, for a time, outweighs the pleasure of possession. The so-called better part is chosen because it is felt to be better.

The hope of future good surpasses the fleeting delight of present indulgence, or the comfort of escape from fear outweighs the value of a momentary enjoyment shadowed by the dread of penalty.

Even the anticipation of happiness far ahead ministers to present enjoyment and gratifies the self.

It follows that, although it may appear impossible to find pleasure in the austerities and privations which some impose upon themselves, the truth is that such ascetics do derive enjoyment from their self-chosen hardships. The claim of special merit for the sacrifice rests on no firmer ground than the credulity of those who, unable to comprehend that pleasure, imagine it does not exist.

The wise may assert the superiority of more solid and enduring sources of pleasure; the far-sighted may praise the permanence of their enjoyment because others are fleeting and deceptive.

Yet no one can honestly deny that he takes pleasure in the way of life he chooses. If he did not prefer it, he would not pursue it. Some value the future more than the present, but even this valuation brings with it the enjoyment of conscious foresight and prudence—an enjoyment no immediate possession can rival. It is a blessing when the capacity for enjoyment is so trained that it responds most readily to worthy and wholesome forms of gratification. The responsibility of those who guide this development cannot be overstated.

The task requires discernment. It is not accomplished by cutting off every questionable source of pleasure and narrowing the field of enjoyment. What is forbidden acquires a special charm, and when the mind, wearied of a few permitted pleasures, gains unrestricted access, there is danger that excess may intoxicate and even destroy.

Parents and guardians err when they seek to secure the future happiness of the young through rigid exclusion. The theatre, for example, becomes an imagined paradise when every visit is forbidden. A moderate and thoughtful acquaintance with it, while judgment is still flexible and open to guidance, would save many an impulsive youth from reckless indulgence.

The same principle applies to all forms of enjoyment that are not inherently harmful.

It is wiser to recognize that such experiences will be encountered, and to prevent them from gaining exaggerated fascination through prohibition. Experience shows that amusements lose their dangerous power when kept in their proper place—neither exalted nor permanent among life's pursuits.

The same truth holds for the many so-called vanities toward which the mind is drawn, often through clumsy attempts to divert it to nobler but less immediately attractive pleasures. It is a grave misfortune when corrupt associations or misguided influence distort the sense of enjoyment and incline it toward genuinely harmful paths.

This frequently occurs when years of injudicious restraint are followed by sudden exposure to the full glare of the world at the very stage when susceptibility is greatest.

It is not difficult to discern a degraded standard of enjoyment prevalent in society at large. Public amusements, fashions, and habits offer abundant evidence of a low moral tone shaping social pleasure.

To lament this condition without seeking remedy is futile. Here lies wide scope for personal responsibility. Each of us owes it to ourselves and to those around us to cultivate enjoyments that rise above the level set by harmful example. The downward tendency is constant and must be steadily resisted.

It is doubtful whether education alone, as commonly conceived, will purify taste or genuinely elevate intellectual power. Coarseness and vice are often found alongside the highest scholastic attainments. Culture of the intellect, by itself, does not ennoble character or uproot moral defects. High and pure views of life may coexist with what is sometimes called ignorance, while refinement of mind may be purchased at the expense of the heart. It is the latter that most urgently requires purification and elevation.

End of the chapter

Chapter-5
The Burden and Illusion of Self-Importance

This chapter explores how self-importance shapes behavior and facial expression. It explains how the desire to be "Somebody" can create pride, anxiety, and pretence, while true worth remains quiet and steady. It teaches that humility, balance, and sound judgment protect us from foolish ambition and help build genuine character.

Fussy faces, careworn faces, supercilious and chilly faces, with here and there a countenance brightened by genuine goodwill and friendliness, commonly take their origin from a sense of self-importance. Consider the mental state of one who goes about with the conviction that the fate of nations largely depends on his intelligence, skill, and patriotism. Whether this belief rests on solid ground or is merely imagined matters little; its effects upon the individual are much the same, and it is with these effects that we are chiefly concerned.

Men and women may almost be divided, by the expression they habitually wear, into two broad classes: the Somebodies, who rule, patronize, or dominate their fellows with more or less grace; and the Anybodies, who submit, meekly or otherwise, to be governed, overlooked, or oppressed. Those who are genuinely content with their place in life, whether high or low, form a very small minority. About their quiet passage through existence—with its modest pleasures and softened sorrows—it scarcely seems worth while to speak, although they are, in truth, the happiest people in the world. Their serenely cheerful faces often glow with a simple ignorance of the most harassing regrets, disappointments, and vexations that disturb human life.

To be Somebody in politics, diplomacy, war, literature, science, art, commerce, or even skilled labor may bring a comforting sense of superiority, but it carries with it a heavy load of anxiety.

Apart from the burden of responsibility, which presses keenly on sensitive natures, there is the constant effort required to maintain the position once attained. Much fluttering and straining of wings is needed to keep aloft above the crowd. The multitude, gazing upward, watches the flight of the eagle and its imitators with curious and critical eyes, and the knowledge of being so observed can scarcely be a source of unmixed pleasure. Triumph itself may be embittered by the consciousness that success has not been achieved without effort that seems ungraceful or forced.

Moreover, to be Somebody implies a claim to deference. If respect is not freely offered—and it often is not—there must be unceasing vigilance to secure or enforce it. Self-assertion may come naturally to certain temperaments, but it must, in some degree, be cultivated by all who would retain a position of prominence. This necessity is a serious drawback to the supposed advantages of self-importance.

The sense of superiority is rarely an unqualified blessing, and those who are spared its temptations may reasonably be thankful to escape the penalties that distinction entails.

At the same time, the absence of this mixed pleasure and pain leaves the insignificant free to indulge a peculiar satisfaction in scrutinizing the virtues, exposing the defects, denouncing the vices, and gently pitying the weaknesses of the great, the prosperous, the pampered, and the favored.

Somebodies, both genuine and counterfeit, abound everywhere. It is difficult to move far without encountering them, and not easy at first glance to distinguish the true from the false. The spurious article often bears the marks of authenticity with surprising confidence, sometimes more boldly than the genuine. This is not strange, for self-assertion is an essential part of the Somebody character, and it displays itself much the same whether the claimed superiority is honest or fraudulent.

Almost anyone may pass for Somebody if he practises the art of deception with sufficient skill. The ease with which the role may be assumed is measured by the readiness of the crowd to be deceived. It is astonishing how readily even sensible people allow themselves to be flattered, misled, and persuaded into surrendering their opinions, their property, their confidence, and even their affections to the adventurous upstart who boldly claims distinction and persistently demands recognition he has not earned. The convictions betrayed, the possessions squandered, the hopes blighted, and the friendships destroyed by such impostures lie at the root of many national, social, domestic, and personal disasters. Hence the urgent need of discernment.

The signs by which genuine worth may be distinguished from pretence are not easily defined. It is often said that imposture betrays itself by affectation, and that the self-assertion of the false Somebody is exaggerated. This is far from universally true. The poorest deceiver is the one who assumes too many airs. More commonly, the successful pretender adopts a tone of humility and self-depreciation. His inward sense of not truly being Somebody assists him in acting the part by restraining excess, while at the same time it sharpens his vigilance. It must also be admitted that many pretenders end by believing in their own fiction. A falsehood repeated often enough may come to wear the aspect of truth even to its author.

Indeed, the pretender sometimes actually becomes, in a limited sense, what he has tried to persuade others that he is. There is a strange power in persistent affirmation to transform appearance into reality. Everyday experience furnishes abundant examples in the world of commerce, where an article scarcely known beyond its promoters becomes, through continuous assertion, a supposed necessity for all. In the same way, a person who is in fact nobody may be made Somebody by incessant self-assertion. Thus is established the ascendancy of adventurous spirits over calmer minds. Mystery plays its part in the process. One who emerges suddenly from obscurity, if he possesses the requisite tact, may gain influence more readily than another whose long and familiar history invites scrutiny.

The sense of self-importance rewards and stimulates the bold and the unscrupulous as well as the worthy. However ill-founded it may be, the feeling itself is real, and it is unreasonable to expect conduct from new men or pretenders that will sharply distinguish them from those who are genuinely eminent. Surprise is often expressed that persons not born to distinction manage to comport themselves creditably in high positions. Such surprise rests on faulty reasoning.

It would be far more remarkable if those who have shown the ability to overcome obstacles and rise above adverse conditions lacked the intelligence to adapt their behavior to the rank they have attained. The consciousness of being Somebody is itself educative and uplifting. It has done much good in strengthening and refining character, even while it has also lent plausibility to deception.

Few things are wholly evil, and the sense of superiority is not entirely so. Yet when self-importance dawns prematurely upon a weak or ill-balanced mind, it often leads to the most absurd and unbecoming conduct. How grotesque is the assumption of intellectual or social superiority when it rests on no solid foundation. The empty-headed adventuress aping the manners of fashion, the uncultivated person posing as a connoisseur, the possessor of mere wealth mimicking the landed gentleman—such figures provoke laughter by their extravagance. The feeling of being Somebody is a treacherous guide. Unless governed by sound judgment, it readily gains mastery over its subject and drives him into displays of folly that are as pitiable as they are ridiculous.

The eccentricities and weaknesses of a great mind may awaken pity, yet they are no less absurd than the follies of a small one. It may irritate us less to be misled by greatness than by insignificance, but the tyranny of imposture is hard to endure in any form, whether it springs from exaggerated merit or from pretension utterly without foundation.

Indeed, human nature seems more inclined to pardon the audacity of a blatant pretender than the overbearing conduct of one whose real worth has been swollen beyond its measure. History appears to show that inflated merit, when exposed, has been punished more severely and more enduringly than hollow pretence, which is sometimes almost forgiven for its boldness.

The sense of importance is also apt to betray its possessor by tempting him to exercise powers he does not truly command. Success in a single field often leads to this danger.

A person who has achieved genuine excellence in one direction begins to think himself Somebody in all directions, and when he attempts to act the part, fails completely. It does not follow that because a man has done something noteworthy he is therefore Somebody in a larger sense.

The diver does not become an aquatic creature because he can remain under water for a time; nor does the salmon become an air-breather because it leaps above the stream, or the flying fish a bird because it skims the surface of the sea.

It is a familiar experience that one who has performed an act of political genius or moral heroism finds himself utterly at a loss in the position to which that act has raised him.

One of the hardest lessons taught by experience is that the power to accomplish an exceptional deed does not imply the capacity to maintain a position of supremacy.

A sense of self-importance may be born of a single great success, but it is more likely than not to end in disappointment. Those are wise who keep this consciousness private long enough to test its foundations before giving it public expression.

At times, however, this sense is present in the mind of a man of genuine ability and sustains him while he performs humble tasks, his talent still unrecognized.

The feeling of power held in reserve breeds confidence, and it is well if it also fosters patience. There is no policy more effective than that of waiting—provided waiting means steady, unobtrusive labor toward a definite end.

He who can wait in this sense will prevail, and nothing so greatly strengthens the self-restraint required for such a course as a rational sense of self-importance.

It fortifies a sound mind against its own impulses, smooths the roughness of privation, encourages reserve, and consoles for many passing humiliations.

This consciousness of fitness for better things and a higher place is not in itself an evil.

The personal task is to use it wisely, to make it serve worthy ends, and never to allow it to gain mastery.

The man who knows himself to be Somebody within a certain sphere—and it is possible to be Somebody in any sphere—will concern himself less with cherishing the feeling than with developing his capacity for future achievement.

Being truly Somebody, it is no hardship, and no sacrifice, to remain unappreciated for a time among present surroundings.

There is then no sulkiness toward the present, no morbid impatience, and none of that theatrical isolation which romantic temperaments and impostors alike are fond of assuming.

The present is regarded as a season of preparation, and every opportunity it offers is valued as a means to an end—means to be used resolutely for both immediate and future gain.

The state of mind in which the sense of being Somebody leads to inactivity is a sure omen of failure.

The idle and dreamy are always ready to shelter their neglect of duty behind the claim of being destined for higher things. Such illusions wither quickly. The clearest proof of unworthiness lies in this form of self-deception. Whoever feels possessed of self-importance and is not thereby stirred to greater diligence and patience is deceived. A lack of purpose and energy is the unmistakable sign of emptiness. Such persons are Nobodies, and from such a condition there is little to hope.

End of the chapter

Chapter-6
The True Meaning of Consistency

Is consistency always a sign of strong character, or can it sometimes be only a show? This chapter explains the difference between true consistency that grows from strong inner values and false consistency that comes from habit or stubbornness. It shows that real consistency is being honest with yourself and faithful to your principles, not simply repeating the same actions again and again.

Few qualities are more widely admired, or less clearly understood, than what we call consistency. To describe a statesman as consistent is counted among the highest compliments, and in every sphere of life the trait is praised, sought after, and envied. Yet, misunderstanding its real nature, men and women often attempt to imitate it by superficial means. They strive to reproduce the outward effects that consistency appears to confer upon character and conduct, forgetting that unless the fruit we admire grows from a sound and living root, it must be hollow and unreal, however fair it may look or however wholesome it may seem.

There is something singularly impressive in a reputation for consistency. It appears to supply the final hallmark of reliability in character. It lends the gravity of age to youth, and gives authority to opinions formed by minds still immature. To say of a person that he is consistent at once commands respect, even from those who may not fully understand his conduct or his policy.

Consistency suggests continuity of action, and such continuity is commonly assumed to be impossible without firm principle and strength of judgment. The consistent person is therefore regarded as one on whom others may rely. The hesitant and self-distrustful gladly follow a leader marked by this quality. To them it seems as though, while they themselves stumble and wander, the consistent individual walks straight ahead with clear vision, having already measured the road, foreseen its difficulties, and resolved upon his course. There is some truth in this belief, but there is also much illusion.

A clever person may acquire a reputation for consistency without possessing any real share of the principles or moral strength which the quality is supposed to represent. This is not said to lessen the value of true consistency. When it springs from genuine sources, it is of priceless worth. Yet, like every other virtue, it may be counterfeited; and considering the high esteem in which it is held, it would be strange if society were not filled with spurious examples—characters decorated with the outward signs of consistency, yet lacking the inner stability and principle that alone make a person worthy of confidence and respect.

Consistency of conduct is one thing; consistency of principle is another. The former has value only insofar as it arises from and reveals the latter. Wise judgment esteems the sign only when it truly indicates the substance. Genuine consistency must lie deeper than appearance. Not infrequently, credit for steadiness of purpose is won by dullness of mind—a level of intelligence too low to be stirred by changing circumstances. Another counterfeit form arises from mere pliancy joined with inertia. Where conditions remain unchanged, the so-called "creature of circumstance" remains the same, and is therefore mistaken for a consistent character.

Viewed with plain sense and a sound understanding of human nature, this kind of sameness should never be confused with true consistency. Lifeless uniformity of thought or behavior usually signals insensibility rather than principle. A failure to perceive the force of changing conditions cannot coexist with that inner strength from which real consistency flows. The person who claims to be consistent simply because he thinks, says, or does today exactly what he did years ago asks to be admired for sheer immobility. As time advances, it is scarcely possible that what suited one's age and circumstances in the past should remain equally fitting in the present.

The consistency that inspires trust is far more than the accident of repeating the same actions under similar conditions. Clay and wax will take the same shape when pressed into the same mold, yet they share no inner principle of form; everything depends on the pressure applied from without. A living organism, by contrast, develops according to a law within itself. External conditions may modify its growth, but they cannot change its essential nature. So it is with human character. The consistency we truly honor is genuine only when it arises from an inner principle—a governing force that stands independent of circumstance and often triumphs over it.

It is of great importance to distinguish between causes so different, though they may sometimes yield similar outward results. Weak or pliable minds may long preserve an appearance of steadiness while sheltered by favorable influences.

Remove that external support, and they collapse, revealing qualities wholly at variance with their former show. Such failure simply exposes the absence of true consistency.

True consistency is inseparable from individuality of character. Here a common misunderstanding deserves mention. Modern thought has tended to exalt the individual as an isolated unit, treating society as a mere aggregation of unrelated persons bound together by convenience or interest.

In this view, individuality is seen as separating and even antagonistic, leading to egoism or eccentricity. This conception is mistaken and harmful, and it is especially important that the young be warned against it.

Genuine individuality is the full and natural development of typical qualities. The finest specimen of a class is the most representative, not the most isolated.

The perfect rose is more completely a rose than one imperfectly formed. In the same way, the best man or woman is more truly human, and instead of being set apart, stands forward as a representative of the order to which he or she belongs. Egoism and eccentricity are distortions of individuality, not its fulfillment. The strength imparted by true consistency reveals itself in the vigorous development of natural and moral qualities. Every distinct trait springs from some latent capacity, and the inner formative force keeps the individual true to his type. This fidelity to inner law is the essence of consistency. It is an active principle of self-respect and self-development, and, in the highest sense, obedience to the rule of nature and submission to the reign of law.

There is little virtue in striving directly to be consistent. Those who make a conscious effort to achieve consistency usually miss it altogether.

It is like trying deliberately to breathe or to exist—processes that succeed only when left to their natural course. True consistency is simply faithfulness to one's better self; it is, in essence, honesty in action.

The imitation that consists in repeating words or deeds merely to align with past behavior is a poor substitute for the real quality. If character were sound and the will loyal to conscience, conduct would naturally be consistent. The same truth applies, with equal force, to consistency of opinion.

If there is no guiding principle in judgment, special precautions must indeed be taken to avoid self-contradiction. But when the mind is its own master, working under that instinctive sense of responsibility and truthfulness which nature implants, no deliberate effort is required to secure consistency. In such a case, consistency becomes the natural outcome of healthy mental activity.

It is remarkable how much labor people expend in striving to appear consistent, and how completely they defeat their own aim in the attempt. The failure springs from the effort itself; it is the penalty of trying to manufacture by artifice what ought to arise spontaneously from sound inner causes.

No sensible person troubles himself to be consistent in matters of appetite. He does not burden his memory with the task of recalling whether he likes beef or plums, nor does he impose upon himself the duty of liking or disliking them on principle. In these matters he trusts nature, and is content to follow its lead. Why, then, should he refuse to rest the obligations of consistency in morals and policy upon the same broad and secure foundation?

The answer is not difficult to find. Human beings live largely for appearances. Conduct is too often artificial, shaped to conform to a preconceived pattern of righteousness, instead of being the simple and honest expression of a pure mind. Where a character is assumed rather than possessed, whether the quality sought be consistency or any other virtue, constant vigilance and effort are required to sustain the illusion.

Hence the difficulty of seeming consistent, and hence the almost inevitable collapse when attention is even momentarily withdrawn from the exhausting task of self-impersonation.

Consistency is not a quality worth pursuing as an end in itself. If it has any real value, it will come unbidden. It would be an exaggeration to call it the highest virtue, but it is certainly one of the surest tests of character. It is often difficult to distinguish what is genuine from what is artificial, what flows naturally from inner order from what is laboriously contrived; but once recognized, a consistently ordered mind is always respectable and generally worthy of praise. It is rare to encounter a person who is consistently bad.

The natural bent of most minds is at least innocent, if not notably virtuous. Hence, when consistency is present, conduct is commonly also sound and creditable.

The true aim of self-culture should therefore be directed not to outward behavior, but to the deeper springs of action. If these are pure and well ordered, the surface of character will take care of itself.

Consistency implies rhythm and order in the expenditure of energy. It is the immediate result of inner harmony.

Actions are coherent, opinions accordant, and policies steady because the motive forces of character work together without friction. Everything moves smoothly when the mind is clear and the conduct consistent, because the heart is right. Physicians tell us that the healthy body performs its functions without drawing attention to any single organ; the effect is achieved while the process remains unnoticed. This truth applies with equal force to the mind and character. A perpetually disturbed moral condition is a sign of disease. The inward conflicts in which some appear to take pride are abnormal. Even when such struggles arise from the clash of good and evil impulses, the evil would never have gained such power had it not been encouraged and harbored in consciousness.

Youth is the season for mastering the passions and uprooting the weeds that choke better growth. If this necessary discipline is neglected, later life will inevitably be troubled by disorder; but the responsibility then rests with the individual himself. Those who would enjoy peace and contentment in maturity must rise early to confront and subdue the enemies of happiness. Consistency is conformity to the nature with which a person is endowed, shaped and strengthened while the mind is still fresh and receptive.

Those who have neglected self-training in youth can attain consistency in later life only through firm judgment grounded in principle. It is never as easy to adopt principle deliberately as it is to allow it to grow into a ruling and inspiring force; yet it is better to aim at principle than to be without it altogether. Consistency can never be made an object without degenerating into imitation. True consistency develops unconsciously, and is usually unnoticed by the person who possesses it. It is a living quality, and therefore progressive. As character grows and changes, so consistency changes with it. It is not sameness, nor is it expressed by the mere repetition of words or deeds. It is fidelity to the principle that governs conduct and shapes judgment—fidelity to one's true self.

This alone is the genuine and worthy form of consistency, the quality all men instinctively respect. Without it, society would become intolerable, clear and effective thought impossible, and life itself a weary and joyless labor.

End of the chapter

Chapter7
Simplicity as Strength of Character

Is simplicity weakness, or is it hidden strength? This chapter shows that true simplicity means honesty, purity of purpose, and a single clear aim in life. It explains how simple-minded truthfulness brings real happiness, builds strong character, and helps both individuals and society remain pure and steady in a complex world.

It is a common habit, especially among the least blameworthy—if not always the most discerning—classes of society, to praise the virtue of simplicity and to speak fondly of childlike simple-mindedness. Yet what, precisely, does this much-used and somewhat ambiguous term mean? Where does its true worth lie, and in what consists its peculiar charm? Half a century ago the language of moral praise was filled with tributes to innocence. Fashion has since changed so thoroughly that the word is now rarely used except with a shade of irony. To call a person innocent today is often to suggest anything but guilelessness.

This change is not merely verbal. It reflects a deeper alteration of feeling, and perhaps even a revolution of thought, regarding the qualities of character that command respect, inspire confidence, and awaken affection in a more complex and exacting stage of moral development. The time has passed when negative virtues—mere freedom from vice—were sufficient to preserve character amid a corrupting atmosphere. Under the conditions of modern life, no simple avoidance of evil, no passive turning away from temptation, no dull indifference to the allurements of wrongdoing, will enable a man or woman to pass untainted through the crowded and restless avenues of existence.

In earlier times a person could, to a large extent, choose his companions, and if evil communications corrupted his character, the blame lay chiefly with himself. Today such choice is scarcely possible. The multitude presses upon us from every side, and it is no small achievement to preserve even a fair measure of individuality. Children are educated in masses; the young of both sexes are thrown together at the most impressionable periods of life, when character is still soft and malleable. Men and women contend side by side in the fierce struggle for livelihood, with little leisure or solitude for the deliberate cultivation of personal qualities. Common needs, common habits, and common customs exert a powerful and often irresistible influence. Under such conditions, something far stronger than mere innocence is required to give firmness and stability to moral character. The instinct which turns instinctively toward simple-mindedness as a safeguard does not greatly err, either in its estimate of the dangers or in its recognition of the means by which they may be overcome.

Simplicity, or simple-mindedness, at its core implies honesty—and no element of character is more indispensable or more effective. Yet few qualities are so poorly understood. Absolute probity is lightly esteemed; perfect truthfulness is scarcely acknowledged as a living moral principle to be embodied in conduct. Even people of high rectitude and sincere intention often content themselves with a loose allegiance to the doctrine that truth is relative, that circumstances justify deviations, and that expediency defines the limits of honesty. To deceive as little as possible, to depart only slightly from a straight line, to adhere to truth so far as convenience allows—this is commonly accepted as sufficient fidelity to duty.

Such a defective view of honesty springs from a lack of simplicity. More than one object is held in view; the moral eye sees double instead of fixing itself steadily upon a single aim. Obliquity of conduct arises from this divided gaze. The primary intention to be truthful is weakened by secondary calculations of advantage and consequence. The firm hold which expediency has upon judgment is shown by the frequent assertion that absolute honesty is impracticable. It is argued that, in the artificial conditions of modern life, outspoken candor would leave the person who practiced it helpless among those less scrupulous than himself.

It may indeed be true that perfect simple-mindedness exposes one to temporary loss in competition with cunning and deceit. Honesty is not always the best policy in the narrow and immediate sense. Yet it remains true that, taking life as a whole, with its balance of gains and losses, strict truthfulness yields the largest measure of genuine contentment and lasting happiness. Those who judge honesty solely by its market value mistake its real worth. Clever evasions, half-truths, and artful concealments may appear useful for a time; but they are short-sighted expedients. In the end, the sacrifice of principle brings regret, and the supposed wisdom reveals itself as both a fault and a folly. The simple-minded refusal of such devices is one of the happiest and noblest qualities, and it ultimately secures the highest reward.

Another fruit of simplicity is thoroughness. Where purpose is single, energy is not wasted. A steady aim, an undivided motive, and an earnest will carry a person forward with fewer hindrances and less weariness than any cleverness of expedient. Instead of being drawn aside by distractions or enticed by the temptations that beset the loiterer, the simple-minded worker does his task and advances steadily. Thoroughness is among the most valuable of human qualities. It lends weight to achievement and dignity to virtue. Many disappointments that darken the close of a career would have been avoided had there been greater thoroughness at its beginning. By concentrating power, thoroughness ensures that whatever is accomplished bears the stamp of completeness, and this alone is a large element of excellence.

Men and women are rarely, if ever, wholly evil. The more thoroughness there is in a character, the greater the likelihood that it will be, on the whole, good. The earnest devotion that gathers all energies around a single aim is usually the expression of a simple loyalty to principle. Moreover, the habit of looking steadily at an object tends to clarify judgment concerning its true worth. Whatever can endure the prolonged scrutiny of an earnest and honest mind is almost certain to be worthy of pursuit. The apparent thoroughness sometimes displayed in evil courses is, in truth, mere obstinacy directed toward a coveted object, not the result of a thoughtfully chosen and consistently followed line of conduct.

Closely allied with thoroughness is purity, another mark of genuine simplicity. Where purpose is single, there is no mingling of false and true principles. The heart remains clear in its affections, and the mind direct in its aims. Impurity arises from divided interests. Corruption begins when sympathy wanders from a single allegiance. It may not be visible at once, but it is already at work when desire turns aside from its rightful direction. This law applies to every form of inclination. Wisdom lies in recognizing the first departure from simplicity of aim, the first surrender of the undivided heart.

No one can serve two masters, and no mind can pursue two rival ends of the same order without forfeiting purity of intention and clearness of thought.

The value commonly assigned to simplicity, or single-mindedness joined with purity of purpose, falls far short of its true worth, whether judged by its influence on the individual or by its importance to society. National character is, in its essence, the sum of personal qualities, with something added that arises from association and the mutual shaping of opinion and policy. If personal character is neglected among a people, a nation cannot long remain distinctive or great. When the tributary streams are polluted, the river into which they flow cannot remain pure. For this reason, it may rightly be held to be the duty of the State, in the interests of public morality, to provide for the moral and religious instruction of the masses, and especially of the young. It is also a powerful appeal to citizens, in the name of the common good, to cultivate personal integrity in all its forms and consequences. Simple-minded honesty and thoroughness inevitably set a high value upon purity, and this, in turn, powerfully contributes to the growth of the virtue so highly prized.

From what has already been said, it follows that simplicity has a fourth prominent feature – individuality. A man or woman who is honest, thorough, and pure, all of which are essentially personal qualities, must of necessity be individualized. Nothing is more worthy of appreciation in art or policy, in conduct or character, than individuality when it springs from the strength of a genuine personal motive, as distinguished from a mere affectation of eccentricity. It has been the glory of the finest periods of art that every true worker has left the mark of his own hand, the impress of his personal manner and skill, upon his work. In every field, genuine excellence is recognized by this sign: the result bears unmistakable evidence of the personal labor that produced it.

This truth is especially evident in the self-culture that grows out of simplicity of mind. Such an individual thinks and acts under the impulse of an inner motive, and the momentum of personal conviction carries him safely past many influences that might otherwise impair his usefulness and weaken, if not ruin, his character. Simple-mindedness is a rare protection against the leveling forces to which all are exposed in the course of life, and under whose pressure so many pliant natures succumb. It seems to set a moral enclosure around the character, guarding it alike from assault and from silent subjugation. The sincerely simple-minded are neither offensively egotistical nor recklessly independent. With a settled purpose and a steady gaze fixed upon their path, they are less susceptible to vague and shifting impressions, and the very quality that gives them individuality saves them from many troubles, disappointments, and regrets.

Simple-mindedness is innocence transformed into an active principle—an ignorance of, and insensibility to, evil that expresses itself in single-hearted devotion to what is known to be right. It is marked by the absence of finesse, cunning, and petty worldly cleverness, and by an unhesitating loyalty to what conscience approves.

It is no reproach to such characters that they are often, perhaps commonly, associated with minds occupied by a single dominant idea.

This is not an inevitable consequence of simplicity, but in its highest form it obeys the maxim, "Whatsoever thy hand findeth to do, do it with thy might." The work may vary and the achievements may be many, but for the time being one object holds the attention, the eye does not wander, and the spirit neither flags nor falters.

Simple-mindedness is a virtue that all should cultivate, and none more earnestly than the young and inexperienced.

A large share of the failures that those far advanced in life look back upon with regret may justly be traced to the absence of this quality. No degree of cleverness, no sharpness of instinct, no devotion to self-interest can make up for the lack of a disposition of heart and intellect that fixes itself steadily on a clearly perceived aim, and shapes conduct as though no rival influence existed to divert attention from the path of duty.

The purity that springs from simplicity brings with it the priceless gift of clear vision, or, what is equally valuable, a firm faith in the ultimate triumph of right, truth, and justice. "To the pure all things are pure," because a single purpose governs the whole field of vision, and whatever lies outside the scope of that pure intention is quietly disregarded.

If there is a royal road to happiness, it is found by the simple-minded. The peace and contentment they enjoy are blessings rarely granted to the restless and calculating adventurer, however well intentioned he may be.

There is only one way by which genuine simplicity can be attained by those who desire its rewards. It is formed of three primary virtues—honesty, thoroughness, and purity—and from these arises a fourth, individuality. Those who would be truly simple-minded must patiently cultivate these qualities, and they must not shrink from the distinctive character that such cultivation inevitably produces.

End of the chapter

Chapter-8
The Foundations of Mental Clarity

Why does the mind give warning signs before it grows weak and confused? This chapter explains the early signals of mental strain and shows the danger of depending too much on habit and automatic work. It teaches that a clear and steady mind comes from protecting brain health and keeping the will strong and active.

The lessons set forth in the preceding papers, when rightly understood and thoughtfully applied, embody the essential principles of healthy brain activity and disclose the true secret of a clear and steady mind.

1. A sense of heat in the head—a burning forehead, a feeling of fullness, pressure, or throbbing—often appears as the earliest warning of mental dulness and confusion. This is the experience that alarms and troubles the worker even before inefficiency becomes apparent. For its relief, almost every remedy is commonly tried except the right one. If this warning sign is examined in the light of a sound understanding of the nature of heat, its modes of production, the conditions under which the temperature of an organ rises or falls, and the means by which it may be most wisely reduced, the sufferer gains valuable help in preserving health. It is only in this practical sense of self-preservation that I seek to render assistance.

2. From a study of habit, the reader may learn to place a just value upon the expertness or so-called "cleverness" that practice confers. He will perceive that it is neither wise nor safe to entrust everything to habit. That form of apparent clear-headedness which consists in relegating most of one's work to automatic processes, while the attention is left free to create the appearance of doing two things at once—a popular and showy exhibition of skill—is neither a great achievement nor a model to be imitated.

He will recognize the fallacy of the common belief that everything depends upon "method," when the term is used in its conventional sense. There is method even in madness, and the most methodical mind may grow feeble by shifting every responsibility and difficulty onto the shoulders of habit, while the will is reduced to an idle attendant on amusement and leisure. The will must remain strong and active, retaining its hold on the serious business of life, directing the mental powers in their proper work, and giving steadiness to the eye, keenness to the ear, and precision to the hand. Otherwise the mind may become disordered, vision confused, perception dissociated from reality, and the creature of habit may discover, too late, that the faculty he trusted most has betrayed him like a false friend.

3. Few influences disturb mental quiet so much as false estimates of time. A true measurement of passing moments, a fair and honest retrospect over the path already traveled, and a clear, far-reaching view of what lies ahead are indispensable conditions of a clear head. I have tried to show how time—past, present, or future—seems long or short, swift or leaden, according to the standpoint from which it is viewed and the mood of the observer. This outline is meant to be suggestive rather than exhaustive, but if it leads the mind into a truer habit of judging time, it will not have been written in vain. In a very real sense, the right estimation of time is closely bound up with mental clarity.

4. The same is true of pleasure. Little sound or enduring work can be done unless the worker finds some degree of enjoyment in his task. It is therefore important that he should understand something of the philosophy of pleasure. With the aim of directing thought toward this inquiry, a few guiding hints have been offered, not as final answers, but as helps toward intelligent reflection.

5. Self-importance ranges from the extreme of empty vanity to that modest appreciation of personal worth which makes life endurable and effort possible. The lesson to be drawn

from its consideration is that the safest and healthiest form of self-consciousness is that which neither depreciates the self so deeply as to destroy confidence, nor inflates the mind with an exaggerated sense of being somebody. Such inflation may rest on no firmer ground than the accident of having done something once that cannot be repeated, or of having gained a position that cannot be securely held.

6. Consistency, as I have sought to show, is a quality of character that must be wholly natural in order to have any real value. It cannot be made an object of pursuit without degenerating into a hollow imitation.
7. Simplicity of aim and single-mindedness in conduct and policy are among the clearest signs of genuine mental lucidity. To do one thing at a time, and to do it thoroughly, is a vital element in the secret we are striving to understand.

Simplicity, or single-mindedness, includes integrity of purpose, thoroughness, directness of aim, earnestness, and individuality. These qualities together form the essential elements of "clearness" as applied to mental or intellectual work.

To apply the principles here set forth is to do all that lies within human power to secure one of the greatest personal qualifications for a useful and happy life—a sound and clear head. The motives and guiding considerations that should inspire and govern the effort to attain this blessing constitute the secret I have endeavored to place within the reader's reach.

The End

www.ingramcontent.com/pod-product-compliance
Lightning Source LLC
LaVergne TN
LVHW100732061126
851857LV00011B/498

* 9 7 8 9 3 7 7 0 7 0 8 5 4 *